Tim Footman **the Noughties**

a decade that changed the world 2000-2009

**crimson**

This edition first published in Great Britain in 2009 by
Crimson Publishing, a division of Crimson Business Ltd
Westminster House
Kew Road
Richmond
Surrey
TW9 2ND

A catalogue record for this book is available from the British Library.

ISBN 978 1 85458 535 6

Printed and bound by LegoPrint SpA, Trento

# Acknowledgements

Thanks first of all to the wise and wonderful Susannah Lear, who had the initial idea then thought I might be the right sort of person to put it into words; throughout the process she offered the gentlest of nudges to ensure the book came in on time and on message. Jim Crawley offered constructive criticism at the early stages, while Andrew Batten's detailed knowledge of sci-fi proved invaluable. At Crimson, David Lester and Lucy Smith kept the faith.

Thanks also to Mary Sexton for her essential Tolworth intervention, and to Laura C, notwithstanding. To Denise, for having the guts sometimes to be bossy.

Thanks to Noel Boivin and Eric DiAdamo who offered nuggets of inspiration, often inadvertently; and to anyone who has hung out at my blog Cultural Snow over the years, especially Fiona Campbell-Howes for giving Chapter 5 a conceptual framework, and Chuck Woww, who identified the cultural significance of Lily Allen. Leonard Cohen and Terry Riley provided the soundtrack.

My parents and the Powell gang remain bedrocks of love, support and comedy gold, as does Small Boo who said 'Yeah, I think you should do it', and I did.

# Contents

# Introduction – A false start

'Two thousand zero zero party over, oops, out of time.'
Prince, '1999'

**Decaditis** (*noun*) the fallacy that 'slicing the past up into periods of 10 years [is] a useful thing to do'[1] (2006)

You are reading a book about a decade. It is not a history as such; it certainly doesn't start at a chronological beginning and move inexorably towards a chronological end. For one thing, as I write these words, the end hasn't even happened yet, although it is within clear sight. Of course, by the time you come to read my musings, this period of time may well be the last decade, in which case it will have become a little more like history, and thus more academically respectable. So, if it's not (quite) history, what is it?

This book is an attempt to find meaning, to identify a few common threads in the events and culture of a time that seemed to hopscotch between life-changing spectacle and mind-numbing banality; between moments of exceptional technological innovation and abject Luddism. It was a period of time that (for most in the developed world) began in an atmosphere of peace, prosperity and celebration but ended in a miasma of brooding global conflict, economic stagnation and confusion.

Although this book is not a history, the subject does crop up occasionally. After all, it was a time when we suddenly realized that 'the end of history', a concept[2] loudly trumpeted in the previous decade, hadn't happened at all. In parallel with this, we found ourselves in a world where the concept of reality was increasingly open to interpretation. History may have returned, but it struggled to keep hyperreality off the front pages. So, if when reading this book you find yourself outraged to discover Simon Cowell or Paris Hilton being afforded more attention than George W Bush or Osama bin Laden, just remember that – for a great many people in the decade – that was a pretty good reflection of reality.

The decade in question, if somehow you neglected to read the sign on the way in, is (or was) 'the Noughties' – though you may not call it that. You might refer to the years between 2000 and 2009 as 'the zeroes', 'the oughts', 'the 2000s' or even 'the ooze'. You might not call them anything particular at all, preferring to wait until society has arrived at some sort of consensus.

It seems we are already operating in a semantic grey area; a 10-year stretch that doesn't have a label we can all agree on. But should we be thinking in terms of decades at all, maintaining the conceit that history fits into preordained slots, which are themselves based upon questionable calculations and approximations of time? As the historian Niall Ferguson remarked; 'A decade is an artificial construct – we're always characterizing them because it's a journalistically attractive thing to do, but these are arbitrary time periods and very few historical phenomena keep like trains to those timeframes.'[3]

So, let's take the 1960s as an example. In purely chronological terms, the decade that goes by that name began promptly on January 1, 1960 and then did the decent thing precisely 10 years later. But that's not what we mean when we talk about the 60s, is it? We mean mini-skirts and flower power, Bobby Moore and JFK. We mean sex and drugs and rock and roll, and that desperately overused footage of a man with enormous sideburns trying on a military jacket in Carnaby Street,[4] don't we?

Following the argument that this kaleidoscope of sounds, images and ideas is 'the 1960s', some commentators have argued that the decade didn't really start until February 1964, when the Beatles appeared on *The Ed Sullivan Show*, shaking the American people out of their collective trauma over the death of President Kennedy. Others suggest that the actual starting point was more like 1958, when the first delivery of sharp-cut Italian suits arrived in London, catalyzing the movement known as 'mod'.

The decade might have ended on time, in December 1969, when a free concert at Altamont Speedway in California, headlined by the Rolling Stones, ended in mayhem and murder. Unless, of course, you hold to the theory that it ended a few months earlier, with the Manson killings, or even that it limped on a few months longer, to April 1970,[5] when the Beatles officially called it a day. Maybe you put the date as late as 1973, when the Middle Eastern oil crisis made the hippy lifestyle financially untenable. Indeed, the idea has been floated that, for most people, what we think of as the 1960s didn't even *begin* until the 1970s, which would mean that a whole heap of golden oldie compilation albums and TV nostalgia shows need new titles.

But the Noughties, as I will be calling this decade over the next hundred or so pages, were different, surely? After all, for centuries the dawn of the new millennium had been fixed in the imagination as a crucial turning point. Of course, it should be noted that this significance was most acute in cultures that follow the Christian, Gregorian calendar; as people in London, New York and Sydney counted down to January 1, 2000, it was 1420 in Riyadh, 2543 in Bangkok and 5760 in Jerusalem. In any case, it seems that the identification of the year 2000 was down to some fundamental miscalculation on the part of the early Christian church; it is now generally accepted that the historical Jesus was born in about 4 BC, and certainly not in December. Moreover, pedants delighted in pointing out that, although the year 2000 had a nice neat ring to it, it really wasn't the beginning of a new decade, a new century or a new millennium at all; in fact, since there had been no 0 BC/AD, that distinction was held by the year 2001.

Still, it was impossible to halt the cultural juggernaut that deemed the transition from 1999 to 2000 as being somehow special. This thinking was inextricably tied up with the millennialist belief that there would be a 1,000-year period of peace before the final conflict between good and evil; that Christ would seize Satan 'and cast him into the bottomless pit, and shut him up, and set a seal upon him, that he should deceive the nations no more, till the 1,000 years should be fulfilled'.[6] As Western society became increasingly secular, this developed into a vague but pervasive post-religious instinct that, if not quite the end of the world, then 'something big' would surely happen when the calendars and clocks flipped over. Prince's evergreen hit '1999' (originally released in 1982) equated the coming of the year 2000 with the Day of Judgement, licensing the preceding year to be one long party. On similar lines, Robbie Williams revealed his existentialist leanings with his 1998 single 'Millennium', which suggested that 'we all enjoy the madness coz we know we're gonna fade away'.

The sense that the year 2000 would signal the end of civilization was in direct contrast to what we had been led to believe by much 20th-century science fiction, which had suggested that on the morning of January 1 we would wake up to a world of personal spaceships and domestic robots. In the film *2001: A space odyssey* (1968), Arthur C Clarke and Stanley Kubrick had presented us with a decade of interplanetary travel and self-aware shipboard computers – although the film's psychedelic *longueurs* (in common with the best futurological imaginings) said more about 1968 than they did about 2001.

These two contradictory perceptions of the coming millennium – crypto-Biblical apocalypse and high-tech paradise – collided in one of the big scare stories of the late 1990s; the 'millennium (or Y2K) bug'.

The tendency of early computer programmers to identify a year with its last two digits meant that there was a risk the year 2000 would be identified as 1900 (or even 19100). Doom-mongers asserted that the resultant confusion would cause ATMs to shut down, hospital equipment to fail and airplanes to drop from the skies across the world. In the event, simple programming techniques were developed to make older computers Y2K-compliant; fallout was strictly limited.

The first big anticlimax of the decade would not be the last, but the Y2K bug bore within it two memes that would define the coming 10 years – technology and fear. As it turned out, there was already another problem in the works, but it was about a different kind of mathematical misjudgement. Since the mid-1990s, investors — especially in the United States — had fawned over internet-related businesses, often without really understanding what they did. New companies spent vast sums on branding and acquiring market share ahead of the competition, in preference to thinking about how they were actually going to make money. Prefixing a company name with an 'e' was akin to dipping it in liquid gold; vague talk of 'new business models' seemed enough to assuage any doubts.

Inevitably, it didn't last. A combination of factors — including a failure to meet projected sales, a US government anti-trust case against Microsoft and some coincidental heavy selling of bellwether technology stocks such as IBM and Dell — caused tremors in the markets, especially on the NASDAQ exchange, where many tech stocks were traded. From March 2000, investors were painfully reminded that bubbles are not only inherently fragile but also hollow; hard reality replaced soft thinking and flimsy economics. Companies such as Boo.com, eToys and Webvan acquired notoriety rather than acclaim, featuring heavily in the 'how not to do it' chapters of business books. Across California's Silicon Valley, technical whiz kids put away the Porsche catalogues and picked up the (suddenly rather thin) job pages.

Although the bursting of the dotcom bubble caused some short-term anguish in the markets, it didn't (as some had feared) provoke a full-blown recession. As one commentator and trader put it; 'The theory that millions of investors from around the world have been systematically stupid for the past six years is simply untenable.'[7] Such faith in the wisdom of those who played the world's markets would persist for much of the coming decade.

But this was in the future. As the year 2000 loomed, all around the world celebrations were being planned to mark the new millennium. In the UK, John Major's Conservative government had set the ball rolling in the mid-1990s, hoping no doubt to emulate the success of the Great Exhibition (1851) and the Festival of Britain (1951).

By the time Tony Blair had become prime minister (in 1997), it was a done deal that the centrepiece of Britain's celebrations would be the Millennium Dome, a vast polyester tent designed by Richard Rogers, situated on the bleak Greenwich Peninsula in south-east London. The opening ceremony for the Dome was a fiasco, with guests left shivering in the cold outside the gleaming new North Greenwich station and Tony Blair linking arms inside the glorified big top with a visibly uncomfortable Queen to sing 'Auld Lang Syne'. Any glitches stood out a mile because, thanks to television, the millennium could be seen dawning hour by hour across the globe, beginning on the Pacific island nation of Kiribati.

Over on the other side of the world, in Sydney, things worked out much better; its magnificent Harbour Bridge gloriously illuminated by fireworks (as was the Eiffel Tower in Paris). In Rio, 5 million people turned out to party on the beaches, while in the US the biggest celebrations were reserved for New York's Times Square. Formerly a byword for seediness and crime, Times Square was now a symbol of the city's regeneration under Mayor Rudolph Giuliani. Once again, the Big Apple looked ready to take on whatever the world chose to throw at it.

For the British, though, it seemed that the musician who had got best measure of the millennium was not Prince or Robbie Williams but Jarvis Cocker of the pop group Pulp, who had realized as early as 1995 that earnest adolescent desires to 'meet up in the year 2000' (as described in his song 'Disco 2000') would inevitably result in crushing disappointment. While the Dome itself was startling in its size and ambition, its content was a desperate mishmash. Tony Blair's New Labour project had declared itself to be both socially inclusive and business-friendly, and the Millennium Experience was a physical expression of these sometimes contradictory philosophies — 14 zones that seemed more concerned with not offending anyone than actually saying anything, each of them sponsored by a corporation. In the centre of it all, acrobats dangled from ribbons in a performance routine that was at once visually compelling, potentially life threatening and ultimately pointless.

The artist David Hockney had suggested that the Dome would be most impressive if left empty;[8] in terms of inspiration and imagination, his wishes were ultimately granted. Those visitors who could be lured to the post-toxic wastelands of south-east London weren't sufficient to prevent millions of pounds of public money being poured into the project, until 'Dome' had replaced 'white elephant' as a succinct analogy for any expensively misconceived public project.

Still, this is not to say that Londoners were completely short-changed by the millennium. The London Eye (which was officially opened by Tony Blair a few hours before his date at the Dome, but not put into operation until several months later) quickly became a popular tourist attraction and landmark, while — a little further downstream — the Millennium Bridge overcame early technical wobbles to become a potent symbol of the city's enduring ability to unite past and present, linking Sir Christopher Wren's magnificent 17th-century St Paul's Cathedral with Sir Giles Gilbert Scott's 20th-century masterpiece Bankside Power Station. In another inspired millennium move, Bankside became the home of Tate Modern. Had Blair hitched his crooked smile to any one of these projects, the dawn of the new decade might have been less embarrassing for him and his government.

Despite the combined efforts of Tony Blair, Jesus Christ and the millennium bug, the new decade had followed the example of its predecessors and obstinately refused to start at the point the calendar demanded. So, when did the Noughties really begin?

To take a view on this we need to delve back into the previous decade, if not further. Actually, not a great deal further, because the 1990s were one of those rare decades that had the good grace to begin almost on time. The destruction of the Berlin Wall in November 1989 had signalled a fundamental realignment of global power, the collapse of the Soviet Union leaving the way clear for the United States to assume the role of the world's sole hyperpower.

Fortunately, the American people had the great good sense to elect appropriate custodians for this strange new era. While the 1980s were personified by the cheerful belligerence of Ronald ('We begin bombing in five minutes') Reagan, the 1990s were ushered in by George HW Bush (as he wasn't known at the time), politically a sort of 'Reagan lite' without the easy charm. In retrospect, Bush's greatest historical significance may not be his own record, but that of his son, who took up residence in the White House for much of the Noughties. In 1992, Bush was ousted by Bill Clinton, who began in a promising manner (the sax, the shades) but saw his presidency degenerate into farce (the sex, the sleaze), to the extent that he made illicit dalliance seem almost boring. In fact, much of the Anglosphere seemed content with tedious government. In Britain, John Major's grey drone came as something of a relief after 11 years of stentorian Thatcherism, while in Australia, Paul Keating paled beside his predecessor Bob Hawke's boozy, weepy blokishness. Keating's successor, John Howard, was duller still.[9]

In the midst of all this tedium, some rather wonderful things happened. In 1990, Nelson Mandela was released from prison, beginning South Africa's transition to multi-party democracy, while in Northern Ireland the Good Friday Agreement was a crucial step towards ending three decades of terrorist violence. There was even hope in the Middle East, with the Oslo Accords between Israel and the Palestinians; though this would prove to be a rather more fragile arrangement.

This didn't mean, though, that the 1990s were a period of perfect tranquility and prosperity. However, when conflict did occur (for example, the wars in the former Yugoslavia that occupied most of the decade and the ethnic violence that tore through Rwanda in 1994), it was usually seen as an isolated event, not connected to the global geopolitics that had defined the landscape since the end of the Second World War in 1945. Even events that would retrospectively be seen in the context of the so-called 'War on Terror' (the 1990–91 Gulf War, the car-bombing of the World Trade Center and the Battle of Mogadishu in 1993) were treated by the media as isolated outbreaks of unpleasantness.

The fear of mutually-assured nuclear destruction that had attended every conflict in the previous 40 years had lifted, to be replaced by a sense of emotional drift among those not directly affected by war or famine. At best, this manifested itself as a feeling of affluent smugness; at worst, as a sense of gnawing unease, similar to the feeling you get when you can't find your keys or think you've left the oven on. We had lived so long under the threat of annihilation that we didn't quite know what to do without it.

Cultural life also lacked a strong anchor; no one piece of footage represents the 1990s in the way that the 1960s or 1980s can be summarized. Grunge, gangsta rap and Britpop all had their moments in the sun, but the dominant musical form could only be defined under the amorphous heading of 'dance' – formless and image-free beyond the nervous grins of a few mega-DJs. Movie stars became *passé*; red carpets the domain of so-called 'Young British Artists' such as Damien Hirst and Tracey Emin, who grabbed the headlines and the limelight as musicians and actors had done in previous eras. The only way to define the 1990s was to contemplate their essential lack of definition. There is a certain elegance in the fact that one of the decade's most successful acts was a band called Blur, and that the most cogent analysis of the time came in a (1999) book by John Robb called *The Nineties: What the f\*\*k was that all about?*

Of course, it is possible to set different parameters. The election of President Clinton in 1992 at least offered a political clean break (the end of 12 years of Republican rule in the US) relatively early in the decade. While in the UK, the 1980s can be closely identified with Thatcherism, which would place the end of that decade at the resignation of the Iron Lady, in November 1990. Still, you could equally well identify the end of the 80s with the UK's ignominious exit from the Exchange Rate Mechanism in September 1992, or the final humiliating implosion of the Conservatives at the general election as late as 1997 (though some might suggest that Blair's reformist New Labour project was just Conservatism in a red tie). As 1997 was also the year in which the rock band Radiohead released their seminal album *OK Computer,* crystallizing the sense of millennialist angst, it is quite possible to argue that the 1990s never happened at all; the decade was merely a history-free buffer zone between the ideological polarities of the 1980s and the socio-religious anxieties of the Noughties.

After a decade of such relentless drift, it was hardly surprising that politicians like Tony Blair wanted to seize on something – anything – that might give their era definition, some hope of reflected glory and glamour. The decade needed a dramatic emotional moment, a visual symbol, to compare with the fall of the Berlin Wall. The Millennium Dome was not the answer, although its lack of impact did inadvertently sum up the 1990s rather well.

Still, when we woke up on the morning of January 1, 2000, we quickly realized that the world had become neither particularly apocalyptic nor futuristic. To all intents and purposes, it was still the 1990s. The Noughties, like all decades, would only start when they damn well wanted. This would happen a little less than two years later, with a defining moment, a defining image, a defining event – more resonant even than the jubilation seen in Berlin in 1989.

# Chapter 1

# Out of a clear blue sky

'They suffered for 102 minutes, the average
running time of a Hollywood film.'
Frédéric Beigbeder, *Windows on the World*[10]

**Impeachment nostalgia** (*noun*) a longing for the
superficial news of the Clinton era (2001)

For eight hours and 46 minutes, it was just a morning, like
any other. All over New York City, people set about their daily
business – going to work, coming from work, walking the dog,
riding the subway; on time, running late. From the Battery to
Brooklyn and Soho to Queens, people talked, joked, worried,
dreamed. Bankers, lawyers, cleaners, tramps.

For eight hours and 46 minutes, if you had asked any one
of these people what day it was, they would probably have
hesitated. They would have known it was September, and
most would have been able to tell you that it was a Tuesday,
but they might have had to glance at the masthead of the
day's *Times* or turn on CNN to tell you that it was the 11th.

For eight hours and 46 minutes, it wasn't even really 9/11.
And then it was, and always would be.

On the morning of September 11, 2001, 19 men hijacked four commercial airplanes flying from airports in the north-eastern United States. At precisely 8:46am US time, American Airlines Flight 11, a Boeing 767 *en route* from Boston to Los Angeles, slammed into the North Tower of the World Trade Center in downtown New York. Seventeen minutes later, a second plane hit the South Tower. At 9:37am, a third plane crashed into the Pentagon, headquarters of the US Department of Defense, in Virginia. Finally, at 10.03am, a fourth plane, United Airlines Flight 93 – which was apparently headed towards the capital, Washington, DC – ploughed into a field in Pennsylvania after its passengers and crew had tried unsuccessfully to wrest back control. In all, nearly 3,000 people were killed that day, the vast majority in the Twin Towers of the World Trade Center; under excruciating circumstances, more than 100 individuals had elected to jump. By 10.28am, 102 minutes after the initial strike, both towers had collapsed.

But you knew all that, didn't you? You probably watched it on television.

These are simply the facts (as we understand them), the bare outline of what happened on that bright, sunny September morning. But 9/11 – as the events of that day came to be known – was to become far more than a collection of specific facts or statistics, terrible as these were. Remarkably quickly, 9/11 morphed into a kind of cultural shorthand; a cry of anguish, a call to arms and retribution, a cliché, even an excuse, whether it was to justify a declaration of war or a downturn in profits. America became 'a nation transformed'.[11] If the country's period of unchallenged political and cultural dominance had begun with one demolition – that of the Berlin Wall in 1989 – it now ended with another. 9/11 was the single inescapable event of the Noughties, and it defined the decade.

Of course, this was not the first terrorist attack on American soil, or even the first attempt on the Twin Towers. Eight years previously, in February 1993, a car bomb beneath the North Tower had killed six people and injured over 1,000. There was also Timothy McVeigh's devastating attack on Oklahoma City in 1995, supposedly retaliation for federal action taken at the Waco, Texas siege. But it was the sheer scale and visibility of 9/11 that sent the American people into a collective state of shock. Apart from the horrifying number of civilian dead – firefighters, office workers, Chinese, Japanese, British, Americans – the whole carefully coordinated event appeared to be a direct attack on US society and policy. America's financial heart, military brain and (if United Airlines Flight 93 had met its mark) democratic soul were under fire. And not from rockets or mortars; planes, not bombs, were the weapons now.

Comparisons were quickly made with the Japanese attacks on Pearl Harbour in 1941 and the assassination of President Kennedy in 1963; this was a real 'Where were you when you heard..?' moment.[12] This time, however, people from across the world had watched events unfold before their very eyes, on television or via the internet. Millions saw United Airlines Flight 175 crash into the South Tower, eradicating any suggestion that the first collision might just have been some horrible freak accident. For days – weeks – following the attacks, there was no other story. Expressions of sympathy and solidarity with the American people flooded in from all over the globe, including from governments whose relations with the US were historically chilly. The headline from the French newspaper Le Monde said it all; 'Nous sommes tous Américains'.

The initial mood among the American people was one of horror and disbelief; 'Why do they hate us?'[13] asked one woman in dismay as she watched the towers lurch and crumble. This was a question asked over and again – in the press, in private conversation or in one of the many blogs that sprung up in response to the tragedy; blogs offering a vital channel to share feelings, experiences and understanding. And it was a very good question. After all, the grim period of self-examination and reflection that had followed Vietnam and Watergate was over; America had won the Cold War, reaching out beyond the Iron Curtain to bring hope, freedom and opportunity to millions. The Americans were the good guys, 'the white hats', John Wayne and Gregory Peck; the Americans were the cavalry. Who would do such a thing?

But this was no time for rhetorical questioning, let alone critical self-examination. All intelligence pointed to the involvement of one Osama bin Laden, the shadowy figure behind a scattered terrorist entity known as al-Qaeda. Bin Laden was (as far as anyone could tell) at large somewhere in Afghanistan – a mountainous, landlocked country at the crossroads of East and West, controlled by the fundamentalist Taliban.

The US swiftly made a series of demands to the Afghan government, including the handing over of any known terrorists in the country and the closure of training camps. These demands were refused, and US forces (along with support from the British) began aerial bombardment of Afghanistan on October 7. In little over a month, the allies had taken the Afghan capital, Kabul.

Back on the home front, President Bush signed into law 'the Patriot Act', which gave US government agencies unprecedented rights of surveillance over the communications and data of its citizens, as well as increased powers to detain immigrants. Objections on the grounds of civil liberties were muted or overruled; there was a war on, after all. And not just any old war in some distant land, something much bigger; this was a war on 'terror'. In this war the enemies were within and without, and they used words and webcams as much as weapons. Not surprisingly, instances of hate crime against American Muslims, Arabs or anyone who even vaguely looked the part began to rise.

Meanwhile, back in Washington, President Bush was enjoying considerable support, his approval ratings soaring past 80%. Global opinion was also (largely) in his favour. The US was reaping the rewards not just of military strength and endeavour but also of a century's worth of cultural and commercial schmoozing; the whole world, it seemed, was wearing Nike, drinking Coke and listening to Britney Spears. Even the language changed, the global media almost immediately adopting the US-style shorthand for the date of the attack (in most countries, 9/11 would usually refer to the ninth day of the eleventh month). For a while, we really were all Americans.

Inevitably, the reverberations of September 11 were felt well beyond the political and military spheres. Artists in all genres were faced with a dilemma; the events were clearly too momentous to ignore, and yet it seemed almost offensive to address them in anything as superficial as a pop song or a Hollywood movie, at least for the moment.

In the weeks and months that followed the attacks, several film-makers confronted a very real practical dilemma; many movies shot in New York were now depicting a city that had, in key respects, ceased to exist — New York still had a face, but its two front teeth had been smashed out. Sam Raimi's soon-to-be-released movie *Spider-Man*, for example, had been trailed by a scene in which the eponymous hero (played by Tobey Maguire) spins a web between the Twin Towers of the World Trade Center so he can snag the getaway helicopter of a gang of bank robbers. The trailer was pulled and the movie's release postponed; images of New Yorkers pelting the Green Goblin (Willem Dafoe) with garbage and Spider-Man juxtaposed with an American flag were hurriedly added to the can. Hollywood, it seemed, was firmly on side.

The comics industry also responded to the events of 9/11. Along with Dark Horse and DC, that most New York of publishers, Marvel Comics (headquartered on Fifth Avenue), produced three titles in tribute. *Heroes* contained 64 full-page illustrations depicting those who had tried to save lives on the day, while *The Amazing Spider-Man* number 36 showed how the heroes of the Marvel universe dealt with the catastrophe; the most poignant panel has the distraught superhuman Captain America[14] being consoled by an ordinary-Joe firefighter. Finally, *A Moment of Silence* contained four (essentially) wordless stories portraying the events of the day from different perspectives; silence perhaps being all there was to say. All proceeds from the publications went to 9/11-based charities.

Among the artistic community, the consensus seemed to be that it was OK – obligatory even – to express the sense of steadfast patriotism that had become the new American *zeitgeist*, but that it was too soon to refer to the specific events that had provoked it. Thus, in the 2002 film *Collateral Damage*, Arnold Schwarzenegger plays a heroic fireman (the New York Fire Department lost 343 personnel in the attacks) who takes on the terrorists who killed his family, ending with an explosive showdown in the State Department in Washington, DC. But the terrorists in *Collateral Damage* are

Colombians not Arabs or Islamists, and a scene in which an airplane is hijacked was cut from the script.

Feelings were clearly running high; there was even an (unsuccessful) online petition to change the title of *The Lord of the Rings: The Two Towers* – the second (2002) instalment in Peter Jackson's hugely popular film versions of the Tolkien trilogy – out of respect for the dead.

There were of course documentaries about the attacks, most notably CBS' *9/11*, which included footage of the first plane striking the North Tower. This was taken by a young French filmmaker who happened to be following a group of New York firemen as events unfolded. But to render 9/11 as something approaching entertainment was still seen as a step too far.

It was not until Spike Lee's *25th Hour* (released late in 2002) that a serious attempt was made in film to address the physical disfigurement of the New York skyline. Lee manages to broach the subject because *25th Hour* is not specifically about 9/11; however, the caustic aftermath of that day permeates the film – the scenes in the apartment of Wall Street trader Frank Slaughtery (played by Barry Pepper) overlooking the twisted, blackened pit of Ground Zero and the corrosive, foul-mouthed monologue of Monty Brogan (Edward Norton) berating every ethnic and social group in New York City, as well as big business, the American government, his friends, himself and:

> ...Osama bin Laden, al-Qaeda and backward-ass, cave-dwelling, fundamentalist assholes everywhere. On the names of innocent thousands murdered, I pray you spend the rest of eternity with your 72 whores roasting in a jet-fuel fire in hell. You towel-headed camel jockeys can kiss my royal Irish ass!

Slowly but surely, Hollywood found a vocabulary with which to address events. A TV movie, *DC 9/11: Time of crisis* (2003), gave the accepted version of the attacks and the events immediately following, presenting George Bush and his government in a generally positive, respectful light. This was welcome news for Bush, whose early months in office had been overshadowed by the narrowness of his election victory in 2000, his success only confirmed after much contemplation of the mythical 'hanging chads' in Florida. To many, Bush's place in the White House was illegitimate. The sudden turnaround in Bush's perceptual fortunes is best summed up by the fact that in *DC 9/11* he is played absolutely straight by Timothy Bottoms, who two years previously had lampooned him mercilessly in the TV comedy *That's My Bush!*

On the big screen, Oliver Stone's *World Trade Center* (2006) focused on various heroic rescue attempts, while (in the same year) Paul Greengrass' *United 93* depicted the fate of the fourth plane (and its rebellious passengers and crew) in real time.

If film-makers were slow to address the events and implications of 9/11, then musicians were positively backward. The telethon *America: A tribute to heroes*, broadcast just 10 days after 9/11, consisted mainly of established stars running through their hits (Billy Joel's 'New York State of Mind', Paul Simon's 'Bridge Over Troubled Water') or cover versions (Neil Young singing John Lennon's 'Imagine', Wyclef Jean with Bob Marley's 'Redemption Song'). These old favourites seemed to set an appropriate tone of comfort, healing and connection. They sustained a sort of therapeutic nostalgia for an America that probably never was, but which many felt to be a safer, better and more innocent place. A couple of newer songs also seemed to catch the mood; 'Hero' by Enrique Iglesias became a radio mainstay in the aftermath of the attacks and

Bruce Springsteen's 'My City of Ruins' — originally written about urban decay in his native New Jersey — would go on to be a key element in the success of *The Rising* (2002), one of the first albums to address post-9/11 America. In a less contemplative vein, Paul McCartney's 'Freedom', premiered in October 2001 at the fund-raising Concert for New York City, appeared to tap into a popular mood for resistance, even retaliation. McCartney soon dropped the song from his set, however, not wanting to be associated with the political and military upheavals that surfaced in 9/11's wake.

But, for the most part, pop and rock musicians were dealing in mood and allusion, writing *around* the subject rather than about it.

Country music singers were more direct. Alan Jackson's 'Where Were You (When the World Stopped Turning)' was a from-the-heart expression of grief at the senseless slaughter. More representative were the gung-ho 'This Ain't a Rag, It's a Flag' by Charlie Daniels and, above all, Toby Keith's 'Courtesy of the Red, White & Blue (The Angry American)' featuring the unsubtle, but cogent, couplet 'We'll put a boot in your ass/ It's the American way'. Keith's balls-out, unrepentant patriotism brought him into conflict with fellow country stars the Dixie Chicks, who derided his song as 'ignorant'. Ten days before the US-led invasion of Iraq, Chicks singer Natalie Maines declared at a gig in London; 'We're ashamed that the President of the United States is from Texas.'[15] The backlash was swift and brutal. In an echo of the response to John Lennon's 'Jesus' remarks almost four decades earlier,[16] American radio stations boycotted the Dixie Chicks' songs and arranged to collect copies of the band's CDs and have them publicly destroyed. It would be several years before the Chicks' popularity recovered.

The Dixie Chicks' problems exemplified the restrictions under which artists and other public figures now worked. Just six days after the attacks, TV host Bill Maher had caused a furore with his appraisal of the bombers; 'Staying in the airplane when it hits the building, say what you want about it, it's not cowardly.'[17] Maher's contract with ABC was terminated shortly afterwards.

Censorship (and self-censorship) was affecting all forms of media. The Scottish rock band Primal Scream, for example, had been performing a song called 'Bomb the Pentagon' during the summer of 2001. What had then sounded like fairly run-of-the-mill anti-establishment bravado now appeared to be a kick in the teeth to the victims of 9/11; by the time the song was released, on the 2002 album *Evil Heat*, it had been substantially rewritten and given the new, rather anodyne, title 'Rise'. Then, on September 11, 2002 – exactly a year after the attacks – artist Damien Hirst came in for fierce criticism when he described the attack on the World Trade Center as 'an artwork in its own right', declaring that 'on one level they [the terrorists] kind of need congratulating, which a lot of people shy away from, which is a very dangerous thing'.[18]

But it wasn't just direct references to the events of 9/11 that had the potential to cause offence. The book *Stupid White Men*, by the American author, film-maker and left-wing polemicist Michael Moore, was scheduled for publication in September 2001. The book's release was delayed following the attacks, after which the publishers demanded extensive rewrites because 'the political climate of the country has changed'.[19] Moore's book included strongly-worded attacks on the legitimacy of George Bush's election victory in 2000, as well as suggestions that he might have learning difficulties and a drink problem. But, essentially, the old partisan hostilities had been put on hold. America was apparently uniting behind its president, and it was only after a sustained internet campaign that *Stupid White Men* eventually saw the light of day. Undeterred by these events, Moore rounded on Bush and his administration's foreign policy when accepting his Best Documentary Oscar (for 2002's *Bowling for Columbine*), going on to lambast the War on Terror in his 2004 film *Fahrenheit 9/11*. Just as contentious was the 2005 independent documentary *Loose Change*, which asserted that the attacks were the result of a US government conspiracy.

Inevitably, the subject of 9/11 soon began to feature in works of literature. The narrators of William Gibson's *Pattern Recognition* (2003) and *Extremely Loud and Incredibly Close* (2005) by Jonathan Safran Foer both lose their fathers in the attacks, while Don DeLillo's *Falling Man* (2007) and Joseph O'Neill's *Netherland* (2008) are both set in post-9/11 New York. *Dead Air* (2002), by the British author Iain Banks, considers the emotional impact of the attacks on the wider world, the book opening with the devastating news from Manhattan interrupting a drugged-fuelled, media-infested party in London's trendy East End. *Chicago* (2007), by the Egyptian writer Alaa Al Aswany, also has a different viewpoint, describing the predicament of Arabs living and working in the United States.

Most of these books engage with the aftermath of the attacks, and its effects on those directly or indirectly involved. Two key works, however, confronted the events themselves. One was *Windows on the World* by the French novelist Frédéric Beigbeder, first published (in English) in 2004. Beigbeder's book focuses on the fate of Carthew Yortston (a fictitious American businessman) and his two young sons who, having decided to take breakfast inside the restaurant at the top of the North Tower, are now trapped. The story of their mounting desperation alternates with Beigbeder's own voice (or a thinly disguised version thereof) trying to make sense of events one year later, atop *Le Tour Montparnasse* in Paris. Some of the most poignant moments in the book come when Yorston tries to convince his young sons that the attack is just a theme-park ride:

> Don't worry, boys, it's all special effects, but I wanted it to be a surprise; it's a new attraction, the plane was a hologram – George Lucas did the special effects, they do a false alert here every morning. Really scared you though, huh?[20]

The other key work to tackle events head on was a (2006) graphic novel by Sid Jacobson and Ernie Colón, based on the official 9/11 report itself. This book created controversy on a number of counts. Some observers felt that the use of such a populist medium effectively downplayed the significance of 9/11, while others felt it was final confirmation that we had retreated to a post-literate age – a world where the masses sit slack-jawed and glassy-eyed in front of a series of spectacular images, deprived of any real context or coherent meaning; which was, to an extent, true.

9/11 was essentially a visual experience – images seen in real time, felt in real time, seared into the collective consciousness. As events unfolded, few were waiting for the next day's paper to tell them what had happened. The news unfurled live on CNN, BBC News 24 and cable; experienced anchors, supposedly immune to shock, mutely joining their viewers in awed contemplation. The focus was on New York (unsurprisingly, the attack on the Pentagon was shielded from public view), the action playing out like a movie. There were few close shots of the individuals directly caught up in events; the image of the fireman labouring up the stairs of the North Tower as shirt-sleeved office workers move calmly in the other direction came a few days later (as did, some time later again, heart-rending recordings of telephone calls made from the burning towers to the emergency services). And Damien Hirst may have been insensitive to say it out loud, but he was right; the images were savagely beautiful, as had been the images of the Challenger space shuttle disaster in 1986 or the burning Vietnamese monk in 1963, Goya's the 'Execution of the Defenders of Madrid' or any number of depictions of the crucifixion of Jesus Christ. Anyway, if these pictures were so ugly, why did we find ourselves compelled to look at them again and again?

But images can deceive just as eloquently as words. Photographs and footage of the Twin Towers belching smoke and aviation fuel, of blurred figures at windows, despairing jumpers and the desolation of Ground Zero, have all become icons; not in the modern, debased sense of the word – where anything from Barack Obama to Hello Kitty can be dubbed 'iconic' – but in the sense of being genuine focuses for communion and contemplation.

If we could go back to, say, September 10, 2001, it might be interesting to ask non-Americans to tell us where (and exactly what) the World Trade Center was. To outsiders, the towers had never encapsulated New York in the same way as the Statue of Liberty or the Empire State Building.[21] The closest the towers had come to impinging on the global consciousness was in 1974, when the diminutive French high-wire artist Philippe Petit had crossed between them, and even then it was the space between the buildings (as well as Petit's antics, dancing fearlessly between the towers no fewer than eight times) that captured the imagination rather than the towers themselves.

A scene from Iain Banks' *Dead Air*, in which various phones start ringing as news of the attacks starts to come through, describes the general response well:

> 'Yo, Phil' I said. Amy answered her call too.
> 'What?'
> *'What?'*
> 'New York?'
> 'The what?'
> 'Where?'
> 'The World Trade Center? Isn't that..?'
> 'A plane? What, a big plane, like a jumbo or something?'
> 'You mean, like, the two big, um, skyscrapers?'[22]

Like James Dean, the World Trade Center looms larger in death than it ever did in life. In a strange way, for many people, it only began to exist after it had been destroyed. 'Reflecting Absence', the name of the official memorial to the New York attacks, throws up any number of paradoxes, chief among them perhaps the apparent impossibility of representing something that isn't there.

Despite its centrality to any understanding of the decade, many artists still tended to skirt nervously around September 11, as if the events of that day were somehow too big to get onto a canvas, into a song or between the covers of a book. As one reviewer of Beigbeder's *Windows on the World* noted:

> It is impossible to write about the World Trade Center attacks and impossible to write about anything else. Novelists who dodge September 11th are doomed to feel cowardly; novelists who take it on are doomed to failure.[23]

Why bother with fiction, seemed to be the general view, when the truth is so much more important? Why bother with fiction, when the truth is so much stranger? The reality of 9/11, or some distortion of it, seemed to play out over and over again. In October 2006, a plane crashed into the Belaire building on Manhattan's Upper East Side. The immediate, inevitable (and entirely understandable) reaction was that it might be another terrorist attack, and the world's news media responded accordingly.[24]

But it wasn't a terrorist attack; it was an accident. Yet, even after this fact became clear, the crash was the top story in newspapers, broadcasts and websites around the planet. This was fair enough in the United States – especially when it became known that one of the plane's occupants was Cory Lidle, a pitcher with the New York Yankees – but the story kept its prominence even in territories with no interest in baseball. For the BBC, *Le Monde*, *La Repubblica*, *Süddeutsche Zeitung*, the *Times of India* and many more, the most important story in the world was not that a plane had crashed but that people in New York City had thought there might have been another 9/11.

Despite all the differences and disagreements (and whether we wanted to be or not), we still all seemed to be Americans. The big question was, how long would this last?

# Chapter 2

# Waging war on an abstract concept

'I just want you to know that, when we talk
about war, we're really talking about peace.'
George W Bush

**Pre-emptive self-defence** (*noun*) an attack before a
possible attack (2002)

One international leader who hadn't joined in the chorus
of sympathy for America's loss was Saddam Hussein Abd
al-Majid al-Tikriti, President (since 1979) of the Republic of
Iraq. Saddam and the United States were worse than enemies;
they were former friends (even if it had been a deeply
pragmatic, opportunistic form of friendship). As an apparatchik
in the Ba'ath Party during the 1960s and 70s, Saddam had
been identified as an influential opponent of communism. By
the 1980s, he had earned the tacit support of the Americans
in his war with the new Islamic fundamentalist leadership of
Iran; though this was a particularly murky affair, prompting

former US Secretary of State Henry Kissinger to declare 'it's a pity they can't both lose'.

It was Saddam's decision to invade Kuwait in August 1990 – on the pretext of a decades-old border dispute – which confirmed his transition from ally to enemy. In what became known as 'the (first) Gulf War', a UN-authorized mission (though one consisting overwhelmingly of American, Saudi and British personnel) got underway. Tasked with removing Iraqi troops and restoring control of Kuwait to its government, the operation succeeded; but no attempt was made to remove Saddam from power in Baghdad.

After the events of 9/11, even old enemies such as Colonel Gaddafi of Libya, Iran's President Khatami and the PLO leader Yasser Arafat expressed their grief, outrage and sorrow. No such comfort issued from Baghdad; 'The American cowboys are reaping the fruit of their crimes against humanity' was the line.[25]

But even though Saddam was no longer a friend of America, there seemed to be little evidence that he was actually involved in the 9/11 attacks. While Saddam was quite prepared to invoke pro-Islamic rhetoric to marshal support among his neighbours in the Middle East, Iraq was essentially a secular republic, especially when compared with fundamentalist hotbeds such as Iran and Afghanistan. In the eyes of theological purists such as al-Qaeda, Saddam Hussein was an affront to Islam.

This did not deter President Bush, however, who seemed determined to finish the job that his father had started. In this he was supported by key advisers of so-called 'neoconservative' persuasion, who stressed America's duty to intervene – with military force if necessary – in the effort to uphold democracy and freedom around the world. Saddam's strident anti-American rhetoric (including heavy hints that he was developing nuclear and/or chemical weapons), along with his continued oppression of opponents and minorities within Iraq, was enough to earn him membership of that elite band President Bush had identified as 'the Axis of Evil'.[26] The invasion of Afghanistan was only the first step in what was to become an ideological as well as a practical battleground – the War on Terror.

But there was a problem. Words such as 'evil' and 'terror' are imprecise and subjective. After all, exactly who decides who is evil, and how can you wage war on an abstract concept such as terror? Whatever terror is – a word, a concept, a state of mind, a feeling – it is *not* a physical entity; it is not a person, an army or a country. You can wage war – and make definitive peace with – a country. This is not possible with 'terror'. Using the term 'war' is also problematic, tending to validate participants on both sides of the ideological divide as 'soldiers'. Even the specific manifestation of terror – the entity known as al-Qaeda – wasn't a coherent organization along the lines of earlier terrorist bogeymen such as the IRA, ETA or the Baader-Meinhof Gang. Al-Qaeda was more of a tendency, a franchise system of essentially independent groupings with a shared ideology but no conventional chain of command.

For various reasons (including, for some, concern that the War on Terror was being used to justify pre-emptive strikes), many countries (including those that had supported the invasion of Afghanistan) were less convinced about invading Iraq. While the United Nations authorized inspectors to search for evidence of 'weapons of mass destruction' in Iraq, it would not condone military action. Setting aside the vociferous opposition expressed by many of Iraq's neighbours in the Middle East (which was largely to be expected), dissenting voices also came from the governments of Russia, France, China and Germany.

So why was the Bush government so committed to invading Iraq? The events of September 11 were clearly a catalyst, but the administration had been making bellicose gestures since Bush took office in January 2001. Even though Saddam Hussein was never explicitly blamed for the attacks, it was clearly politically expedient to allow rumour and conspiracy theory to fester among the American people. A general lack of knowledge and curiosity about the complex politics of the Middle East made this easier; as late as 2006, 85% of US servicemen in Iraq declared that their main mission was to 'retaliate for Saddam's role' in 9/11.[27] The fact that no such role existed was pretty much irrelevant.

That being said, there was genuine unease about Iraq's military capabilities and ambitions, in particular its supposed possession of weapons of mass destruction; although, in the event, these were not discovered.[28] Still, there could be no doubt about the Iraqi regime's dire human rights record, although (for some) the US had a long record of overlooking such matters when wider geopolitical considerations were in play.

Opponents of US policy, along with non-aligned cynics, pointed to the commercial links between the Bush administration and the oil industry, with particular reference to Vice President Dick Cheney's links to the oilfield services corporation Halliburton. But the real reason for the invasion of Iraq might go even deeper. Back in the 1980s, when speaking to American journalists during the weapons negotiations that would eventually lead to the collapse of the communist bloc, a Soviet foreign policy advisor called Georgi Arbatov had commented; 'We are going to do the worst thing we can do to you; We are going to take your enemy away from you.' And he was right; ever since the fall of the Berlin Wall, America had lacked a coherent focus for its fears. Now, in the aftermath of 9/11, the American Superman needed a few Lex Luthors to take the blame.

In 2002 and the early part of 2003, the rightness or otherwise of action against Iraq began to polarize political and cultural opinion, just as the Spanish and Vietnam conflicts had done many decades before. A key difference this time round, however, was that the debate became heated long before a single shot had been fired. It was also an argument that didn't split on traditional battlelines of left and right. Although President Bush presented himself as a conservative, several of his administration's key cheerleaders for Iraqi 'regime change' (an elegant euphemism for the removal of Saddam) were neoconservatives, many of whom held left-liberal views on issues other than foreign policy. Maverick right-wingers such as Pat Buchanan and Ron Paul opposed the invasion, while many Democrats (Joe Lieberman and Zell Miller among them) supported it. In Europe, the nominally left-of-centre Tony Blair was for the invasion; the right-of-centre Jacques Chirac, President of France, against.

The situation in Europe was complicated by the fact that many countries – in particular Britain, France and the Netherlands – had a substantial Muslim population, proportionately far larger than that in the US. Social unrest among the UK's Muslim community had broken out before, in 1989, when the Iranian government had issued a fatwa against author Salman Rushdie for his depiction of the Prophet Muhammad in his (1988) novel *The Satanic Verses*.

As the arguments for invading Iraq became increasingly entwined with the broader conflict with Islamist terrorism, tensions began to rise. This made for some interesting rearrangements of political viewpoints. Rushdie's fellow British novelists Martin Amis and Ian McEwan – who might normally have been expected to sign up to an anti-American left-liberal consensus – were more ambivalent about the advisability of an invasion, citing the conflict between Islamism and free expression. Issues of religion clouded matters further. While the American religious right – a key political constituency for Bush – was almost unanimously in favour of the invasion, things were less clear cut elsewhere. The atheist and liberal polemicist Christopher Hitchens became a vociferous supporter of action against Saddam; Peter, his conservative Christian brother, opposed it. In the UK, the renegade anti-war politician George Galloway formed a new left-wing party, the Respect coalition, creating an unlikely (and briefly successful) alliance between Trotskyists and socially conservative Muslims.

February 15, 2003 was witness to mass coordinated anti-war demonstrations in hundreds of cities around the world. In London, former carpenter Brian Haw continued his highly visible one-man anti-war protest in Parliament Square. So visually arresting was Haw's display that, in 2007, artist Mark Wallinger meticulously reconstructed it for an installation at Tate Britain. Haw's colourful protest was a constant source of embarrassment to the British government and, in a controversial move, finally prompted a ban on all unauthorized demonstrations within a half mile of the Palace of Westminster. In order to protect our democratic freedoms, it seemed, it had become necessary to curtail them.

Despite the protests, the momentum for invasion was all but unstoppable. When troops did finally move into Iraq, in March

2003, it was almost an anticlimax. Iraqi forces were unable to stage any kind of meaningful resistance, and the US-led coalition soon had the upper hand. Saddam's feared sons Uday and Qusay were quickly dispatched, and images of a statue of Saddam being pulled down and thrashed with shoes were beamed around the planet. A pro-Western government was hurriedly installed. At the end of 2006, Saddam (who had been discovered hiding out near his home town of Tikrit) was hanged. Camera-phone footage of his death made the whole thing seem even more sordid.

So one perceived threat to peace and prosperity had been eliminated; but the invasion of Iraq had hardly made the world a safer place for liberal democracy. One of the first actions of the Coalition Provisional Authority (in May 2003) had been to disband the Iraqi army, which immediately put 250,000 armed, unemployed men on the streets. Extremist Islamism, which had been a marginal presence in Iraq under Saddam, began to flourish as al-Qaeda operatives took advantage of the chaos. Where Iraqis had once lived in fear of the capricious wrath and paranoia of Saddam Hussein's dictatorship, they now had to contend with gun attacks, car-jackings and suicide bombers.

Not that this was confined to Iraq. While America itself had been spared a repeat of the events of 9/11, terrorist attacks continued elsewhere in the world. In October 2002, on the Indonesian island of Bali, members of the Islamist organization Jemaah Islamiyah detonated three bombs, killing 202 people and wounding over 200 more. The pro-war camp hailed the attacks as evidence of the continuing threat of terrorism; opponents, on the other hand, argued that such attacks were provoked by the continuing support certain governments offered George W and Bush. The main target of the Bali bombings appeared to be tourists from Australia, whose government was staunchly pro-invasion.

Then, in March 2004, a series of coordinated bombings on rush-hour commuter trains headed for the Spanish capital Madrid killed 191 and injured nearly 2,000. Spain, like Australia, was an ally of the invasion coalition. The fact that this event took place three days before the country's general election was interpreted as an attack on democracy; the fact that the anti-war Socialist Party won the ballot suggested that the support for US policy espoused by ousted Premier José Maria Aznar was not widely shared by the electorate.

Terrorist violence or (almost as importantly) the perceived threat of such violence became a menacing presence in many Western cities. Author Ian McEwan discussed this in 2005 when promoting his novel *Saturday*, set in London on the day of the anti-war protests:

> Slowly I began to think, if I'm writing this London novel and it's in the present and about the present, then it needs to be about what was going on. And what was going on was the post-invasion of Afghanistan and the lead-up to the invasion of Iraq. And a colossal nervousness after the Bali bombing and even before Madrid. A general sense in European cities, and I guess in the US too, about when the next shoe would drop. We were assured that it was inevitable, and I know they were covering their backsides by saying it, but still, it got into the small print of private life.[29]

A few months after *Saturday* was published, the shoe did indeed drop. Shortly before 9 o'clock on the morning of July

7, 2005, four bombers blew up three trains on two different lines of the London Underground system; about an hour later, a fourth device went off in Tavistock Square, on a number 30 bus to Hackney. In all, 56 people (including the bombers) died and over 700 were injured. London had its own 9/11, or rather, 7/7.

Unlike 9/11, however, the 7/7 attacks were not primarily a visual experience. The London attacks were largely played out far from public view; three out of the four explosions occurred underground. The terrifying beauty that Damien Hirst had seen in the images from New York wasn't replicated in the pitch-black tunnels. Instead, it was a golden opportunity for so-called 'citizen journalism', with blurry camera-phone footage of passengers walking along tube tracks. The most arresting image the mainstream media could come up with was the bus, its roof peeled back like a can of sardines. Only later came CCTV footage of the four young bombers, explosives weighing down their rucksacks, boarding trains bound for the capital.

While Americans had watched the events of 9/11 unfold on television, many Londoners pieced together the events of 7/7 via radio. Jon Gaunt, the closest thing British radio has to an American-style right-wing shock jock, was hosting his regular morning phone-in programme on BBC London, celebrating the city's success in securing the 2012 Olympics – a decision that had only been confirmed a few hours previously. At about 9.25am, calls started coming in from listeners to say that there was something going on at Edgware Road station; then another call, there was something going on at King's Cross. It was hard to say exactly what was going on at this stage (was it perhaps a power surge?), but as the show progressed there were further calls from observers and witnesses; we even heard the words of victims. By around 11.30am, the giant electronic driver-information displays which hang over the main routes into the British capital were flashing the terrifying message 'Avoid London. Area Closed'.

But the shutdown didn't last for long. Once the initial shock had faded (and distrust of young swarthy men carrying outsized luggage on the Tube had abated), Londoners expressed their resistance, not with an outpouring of grief but with a slightly sardonic insistence on 'business as usual'. Websites sprang up with Londoners wielding the slogan 'I Am Not Afraid' and an old poster from World War II, emblazoned with the words 'Keep Calm and Carry On', became newly fashionable. Memories of terrorist atrocities perpetrated by groups such as the IRA resurfaced, and a grim collective determination not to be bowed by adversity prevailed. What most appalled many, however, was that the London attacks had not been perpetrated by some hostile, external force but by young *British* Muslims; this attack was home-grown. And it wasn't the end of it. Two weeks later, a further set of coordinated attacks on London failed; and in 2007, two men drove a propane-laden jeep into the terminal of Glasgow Airport, although the only fatality was one of the attackers.[30]

In 2005, a Danish newspaper published 12 cartoons (most of which depicted the Prophet Muhammad), supposedly as part of a debate on multiculturalism and self-censorship. As the images were printed in other countries, they were followed by increasingly noisy protests, many of them stirred up by extremist clerics who exacerbated the situation by adding a few more images to the original dozen. Danish goods were boycotted, embassies were attacked and more than 100 people were killed.

Suddenly there was a wariness about anything that could be perceived to insult religion, especially Islam. Sometimes this was expressed as a new-found sensitivity to religious and cultural feelings, but just as often it was a desire not to be blown up. In London, Tate Britain refused to display an installation by John Latham that depicted copies of religious books (including the Qur'an) embedded in a 6-foot sheet of glass, while in Birmingham, protests forced the closure of a play held to be disrespectful to Sikhs. Elsewhere, Hindus protested against paintings that supposedly denigrated their deities, while Christians protested against a TV version of the subversive musical *Jerry Springer: The opera*. Even Saddam Hussein got in on the act, when a gallery in Belgium was forbidden from displaying a life-sized model of him floating in a tank of formaldehyde.

In fact, the whole situation was extremely disconcerting and complex, which perhaps explains why television took some time to address the issue that lay behind it – the war in Iraq. The short-lived series *Over There* aired in 2005, while we had to wait until 2008 for *Generation Kill*, an adaptation of Evan Wright's 2004 book of the same name. Chronicling his experience as an embedded reporter with the US Marines, Wright's book joined Ian Ewan's *Saturday* (2005), John Updike's *Terrorist* (2006) and Mohsin Hamid's *The Reluctant Fundamentalist* (2007) as key literary markers.

But you didn't need to read a book to know there was something serious going on. Flashpoints such as the cartoon controversy, along with the attacks on London and Madrid, combined to make the conflict in the Middle East a reality for ordinary people living in the West. This wasn't about tracer bullets in the desert sky or shells raining down on a city the name of which we couldn't pronounce; this was about places we knew and people we thought we understood. The attacks galvanized public debate; people clearly wanted to understand this conflict, and why it was provoking so much outrage. The problem was, it was turning out to be a fiendishly difficult subject to pin down.

Neither side in the argument helped matters. Supporters of the invasion never seemed able to agree whether it was about terrorism or chemical weapons, human rights, oil or some combination of the above. Similarly, opponents' claims were clouded by arguments about Palestine, global capitalism and, in some cases, a desire to wipe the self-satisfied smirk off George Bush's face. The President's image was in fact widely lampooned in the conflict; cartoonists variously depicting him as a trigger-happy cowboy or a feeble-minded ape. What rankled most (even with many of his instinctive supporters) was that Bush seemed to see the conflict in such simplistic, black-and-white terms. Bush's appearance as early as May 2003, under a banner screaming 'Mission Accomplished', suggested a man with an idiosyncratic grasp of reality, to say the least.

Small wonder mainstream media outlets – which at least tried to maintain a degree of objectivity – found themselves losing readers, viewers and listeners throughout the decade. Far more successful were outlets such as the red-bloodedly pro-war Fox News and the Arabic network Al Jazeera. The conflict also coincided with an explosion in political blogs, many of which attached themselves to one ideological position, and then flogged it mercilessly.

Desperate to claw back lost ground, the old-style media resorted to presenting the conflict as they might a celebrity talent contest, in terms of image and personality. The big players – Bush and Blair, bin Laden and Hussein – were constant presences across all media, but they faced an ever-changing line-up of competitors. Some of these figures were already well known, such as Rudy Giuliani, the Mayor of New York on 9/11, whose post-attack walkabouts and stirring, *ad hoc* pronouncements embodied the city's determination to recover from trauma.[31] Most, however, were more obscure, for example Valerie Plame, a CIA officer whose cover was blown in mysterious circumstances when her husband, a former diplomat, queried some of the US government's justifications for the invasion of Iraq. Some were simply in the right place at the right time; the British author Chris Cleave, for example, whose novel *Incendiary* (about a fictional terrorist attack on London) was published on the day of the real attacks and garnered considerable publicity. Others were less fortunate; the American journalist Daniel Pearl and the Dutch film-maker Theo van Gogh, both murdered by Islamist extremists, and a Brazilian electrician, Jean Charles de Menezes, shot dead by British police who mistook him for a terrorist suspect.

Sometimes the media became the message. This was the case in 2003 when a BBC radio journalist named Andrew Gilligan suggested in a live broadcast that the British government had deliberately 'sexed up' an official dossier about Iraq's military capabilities, specifically the contention that Iraq was capable of deploying chemical weapons within 45 minutes of an order so to do. The Blair government, especially its outspoken Director of Communications, Alastair Campbell, responded with fury. Following an official enquiry, Gilligan, along with Greg Dyke (the Director General of the BBC) and the Chairman of Governors, were all forced to resign. Dr David Kelly, the weapons expert identified as the source for Gilligan's story, was found dead in woodlands near his home. Kelly's death was officially determined to be suicide, but this did not deter the conspiracy theorists. Similar rumours attended the death in 2005 of Robin Cook, the former Foreign Secretary, who had resigned from government in protest over the decision to invade Iraq.

All these faces flickered in and out of the picture, but Osama bin Laden (albeit in virtual form) remained on screen. The hunt for bin Laden had been cited as one of the reasons to invade Afghanistan, but as the decade wore on he proved eminently resistant to capture. US sources alternated between condemning him as the most dangerous man on Earth and questioning whether he was alive or dead. As US Defense Secretary Donald Rumsfeld noted in 2002; '[Osama bin Laden is] either alive and well, or alive and not too well, or not alive.'[32] Meanwhile, bin Laden (or someone who looked very much like him) made sporadic video appearances, vowing retribution against America, Israel and their allies before fading back into the caves he supposedly called home.

Low-quality footage of a mysterious man with a beard may have been useful for American moms seeking a bogeyman with which to frighten recalcitrant children, but as the military action in Afghanistan dragged on it became clear that this wasn't enough to maintain the overwhelming public support Bush had enjoyed in the aftermath of 9/11. Instead, the focus was on less coherent threats – that old favourite 'terror', or a new coinage – 'Islamofascism'. Clearly, these were bad things, but they were harder to convert into an electoral *piñata* than either a new Hitler or a second Stalin would have been. If bin Laden wasn't going to stand still long enough for American forces to apprehend him, someone else would have to take the rap.

Fortunately, the Americans had a fertile source of bad guys close at hand. Guantánamo Bay, an area on the southern tip of Cuba that was permanently leased to the US government, had become home to a detention camp. As the campaigns in Afghanistan and Iraq progressed, the camp began to fill with prisoners. The precise status of these men depended on circumstances (and to whom you were talking) – they were either terrorists, prisoners of war, freedom fighters, dissidents, confused idealists, political prisoners, martyrs, murderers or merely simpletons in the wrong place at the wrong time. The characteristic orange jumpsuits the inmates all wore reduced them to the status of faceless, identity-free nobodies, the collective representation of terror (or, if you preferred, of America's dehumanization of its enemies). Pretty soon the suits became acceptably ironic garb for student fancy dress parties.

As the general perception of the War on Terror shifted, so too did the image of the inmates at Guantánamo Bay. Because the War on Terror wasn't a conflict with a defined end point (how can you defeat an abstract concept?), there was no generally accepted process for dealing with the prisoners. Should they be tried? Transferred to normal US prisons? Court-martialled? Held indefinitely? Returned to their homes? Executed? Even observers who accepted that many of the individuals were in some way involved with terrorism, condemned the situation as being poorly thought through.

Questions also began to arise about exactly how the inmates were being treated. A new euphemism entered the political lexicon – 'extraordinary rendition', the process of transferring prisoners to territories outside the jurisdiction of the United States where legal constraints on interrogation and torture were somewhat more lax. In fact, the American authorities at Guantánamo seemed to be waging a parallel war against the English language; when (in June 2006) three inmates committed suicide, a senior officer described it as an act of 'asymmetric warfare'.[33]

But conditions in Guantánamo were nothing compared to the horror stories coming out of the Abu Ghraib prison in Baghdad. The use of chains, dogs and sexual assault on prisoners undermined the belief that the US-led coalition represented the good guys, no matter how many euphemisms for torture spokespeople could come up with. It was difficult to know what reflected worse upon the US military personnel running the facility; that they were barbaric enough to inflict such degradation upon the prisoners under their charge or that they were stupid enough to have the whole thing captured on camera. Rumours persisted of even more damning photographs, reinforcing the belief that Lynndie England and Charles Graner (the soldiers who received the longest prison sentences) were effectively scapegoats.

In truth, the detainees – like so many other facets of the War on Terror – were proving to be a millstone around the neck of George W Bush. The increase in the number of US troops in Iraq in 2007 (a process generally referred to as a 'surge') reduced levels of lawlessness and insurgency but didn't return the country to anything that could reasonably be described as peace. The coalition wasn't exactly losing to al-Qaeda and its supporters, but it wasn't exactly winning either. The only feasible response was a permanent state of crisis management. With tactical deadlock abroad, and a worsening financial situation at home, Bush's approval ratings slumped to humiliating levels during his second term.

In the 2008 election, the Republican nominee John McCain was decisively beaten by a bright young Democratic senator from Illinois named Barack Obama, who campaigned on a platform of withdrawing US troops from Iraq.

When, in December 2008, an Iraqi journalist hurled his shoes at Bush during a press conference, it seemed a fitting end to the President's time in office. Not that his successor possessed a magic wand that could rid the world of terror; at the end of November, only a few weeks after the election, 173 people died in a coordinated series of bombings and shootings in the Indian city of Mumbai.

In January 2009, newly-elected President Obama announced plans to close the detention camp at Guantánamo within the year. However, in May 2009, he decided against publishing photographs detailing abuse of Iraqi detainees at Abu Ghraib and elsewhere on the grounds that they would put American troops at increased risk.

At the time of writing, Osama bin Laden remains at large, and he probably will be for some time. It remains to be seen whether President Obama finds him a useful enemy.

## Chapter 3

# Is it me or is it getting hot in here?

'What changed in the United States
with Hurricane Katrina was a feeling that
we have entered a period of consequences.'
Al Gore

**Global weirding** (*noun*) an increase in unusual
environmental activity, often attributed to climate
change (2007)

As we inched our way towards a new decade and a new
century, many felt a palpable sense of relief that we had got
this far; that the world as we knew it hadn't come to some
terrible, shattering end. The threat of nuclear annihilation that
had hovered since the 1950s had largely disappeared with the
collapse of the Soviet Union, and we now looked ahead to the
millennium with a sense of both hope and dread. However,
as we finally entered the year 2000 – and realized that the
combined forces of John of Patmos, Nostradamus and the
Y2K bug had not in fact laid waste to human civilization –

people began to look around for something new to get worried about.

Of course, for many in the West, the spectre of global terrorism was more than enough to cause concern. This often manifested itself as a persistent undertone of nervous paranoia – why was the guy in front buying so much weedkiller; was it to make home-made explosives? Was there a lethal pathogen hidden in that shampoo bottle? Airports took the terrorist threat particularly seriously, air travel becoming an increasingly fraught experience as closer security checks and baggage protocols provoked queues, cancellations and delays from JFK to Tullamarine.

But an even deeper fear permeated the Noughties, one that threatened not simply to turn the world as we knew it upside down but effectively to destroy it. Since the 1980s, scientists had become increasingly concerned by a slow but insistent rise in the average temperature on the Earth's surface. Left unchecked (they calculated) this would have dire environmental effects, including droughts, floods and the permanent swamping of coastal areas by rising sea levels. Major cities such as London, New York, Mumbai and Tokyo might ultimately be at risk of inundation. Conversely, Adelaide – Australia's fifth biggest city – risked desiccation as higher temperatures and the continued fall in the flow of the Murray River took their toll.[34] To cap it all, the chief culprit for all this trouble seemed to be humanity itself; specifically, the excessive production of carbon dioxide caused by burning oil and coal, which kept heat in rather than letting it escape into the atmosphere – the so-called 'greenhouse effect'.

Still, global warming is nothing new. The world has been convulsed by changes in temperature (both warming and cooling) for millennia; you could, for example, grow grapes and apricots in the south of England in the 15th century, and that was long before industrialization made its mark. What was different this time round was that now we could measure and predict any change on a global scale, and extrapolate its effects. And it seemed it wouldn't take much for the Earth to pass a crucial 'tipping point' – a rise of just 2°C above pre-industrial levels.

This was a story too good to be missed, and publishers responded with a raft of new titles. Mark Lynas' *Six Degrees* (2007) detailed the effects on different ecosystems of apparently small, incremental rises above the average temperature of the Earth. And it was not a pretty picture; according to Lynas, a rise of just 1°C would mean the loss of most of the world's coral reefs, while a three degree rise would spell the collapse of the Amazon rain forest, the disappearance of Greenland's ice sheet and the creation of deserts across the mid-western United States and southern Africa. Don't ask what would happen at six degrees.

While Lynas focused on cause and effect, others – such as George Monbiot in his book *Heat* (2006) – explored possible solutions, including (controversially) massive reductions in air travel. Still others took the personal improvement route, urging us to 'detox' or 'decarbon' our lives. One outlier success was academic David MacKay's book *Sustainable Energy* (2008). Published without the benefit of a snazzy jacket or massive promotional push, MacKay's book nonetheless caught the eye, its accessible tone prompting influential blog Boing Boing to note; 'This [book] is to energy and climate what *Freakonomics* is to economics.'

Fiction writers also took up their pens, the distinguished Canadian author Margaret Atwood publishing her dystopian novel *The Year of the Flood* late in the decade.

Everywhere you looked, thousands of tons of paper were being turned into books about global warming – all from sustainable forestry, naturally.

The theatre also had its say, with plays such as Steve Waters' *On the Beach* and *Resilience* (2009) presenting the issues in compelling human terms. Meanwhile, in the visual arts, Angela Palmer exhibited a variety of media – film, photography, found objects and vials of air – from her travels to Linfen in Shanxi province, China (said to be the most polluted place on Earth) and Cape Grim on the north-west tip of Tasmania (said to be the least polluted). Two previously identical white outfits she wore in both locations were also exhibited.

Despite all this artistic activity, it is worth remembering that concern for the environment is not a new obsession. People have been worrying about the effect of human progress on the natural world since the dawn of the Industrial Revolution in the late 1700s. It was not until the late 1960s, however, that 'environmentalism' became a coherent force in politics and society. The back-to-nature aspects of the hippy movement, coupled with a more generalized concern about an overreliance on nuclear and fossil fuels (exacerbated by the 1973 oil crisis and the OPEC oil barons), led many people to question whether economic and technological development was always a good thing. In a piecemeal way, this thinking began to affect public policy – for example, the removal of chlorofluorocarbons (CFCs) from aerosols and refrigerators to prevent further erosion of the ozone layer, and the introduction of unleaded petrol after links were discovered with illnesses in children.

As far back as 1962, Rachel Carson's hugely influential polemic *Silent Spring* had highlighted the detrimental effects of pesticides on the environment, kickstarting the American ecology movement and facilitating the eventual banning of DDT in the United States. Eleven years later, EF Schumacher's *Small is Beautiful* had provided an ideological basis for the various campaign groups and green political parties that erupted in the 1970s.

Writers of fiction were also inspired. In 1962 (the same year that *Silent Spring* was published), JG Ballard's sci-fi novel *The Drowned World* presented an apocalyptic vision of a planet under water after the polar ice caps had succumbed to solar radiation. Ten years on, Richard Adams' bestselling allegorical novel *Watership Down* (later an animated film) chronicled the journey of Hazel, Fiver and a group of fellow rabbits as they fled the destruction of their burrow by greedy land developers.

The resurgence of popular capitalism in the 1980s and 1990s made such ecological glumness a little less fashionable, although there always seemed to be an apocalyptic blockbuster around the corner. Some, such as the *Mad Max* trilogy (1979–1985), were successful; others, such as the idiotic and hugely over-budget *Waterworld* (1995), less so. All this was to change in the Noughties, as issues around the environment loomed ever larger in the public consciousness.

The spectre of global warming presented some stark choices. Redesigning hairspray cans or tweaking car engines to run on unleaded petrol had been relatively painless adjustments. But the global warming crisis struck at the heart of what many people took for granted as part of modern life – door-to-door car travel, low-cost flying and strawberries out of season. Suddenly, middle-class consumers started totting up 'food miles' as well as calories. It wasn't enough simply to remove certain forbidden fruit from our shopping trolleys, the way many people had avoided South African oranges during the apartheid era; this was something that would touch every aspect of our lives. Discussing one's carbon footprint became acceptable dinner party conversation; recyling, freecycling and even car boot sales newly fashionable.

But being 'eco-friendly' was a deeply fraught business. Exactly how many trips to the bottle bank would offset that trip to Barcelona or Florida? Would it be better to buy a newer, more fuel-efficient car or stagger on with the old one to avoid the environmental impact of manufacture? Should it be local, factory-produced 'Cheddar' or organic Taleggio flown in from Italy? These deliberations provoked as much hot air as they were intended to prevent; there was no easy answer.

Meanwhile, for some, there was also simply no case to answer. A small but vocal *cadre* continued to argue that global warming wasn't really happening or, if it was, there wasn't a lot we could do about it. Others – most notably the Danish economist Bjørn Lomborg in his 2007 book *Cool It* – argued that our resources might be better spent on more immediate problems, such as fighting HIV/AIDS and ensuring safe water supplies.

Inevitably, much of the denial rhetoric came from members of the pro-business political right, who saw the issue as a threat to their prosperity. President Bush, with his background in the oil industry, was widely seen to be dragging his heels. But some on the left were also sceptical about wholesale carbon reduction, concerned about the effect that rigorous environmental legislation might have on developing econo-mies, particularly India and China. The Western world had enjoyed the benefits of unfettered oil use for decades but was now seen to be withholding these boons from others. The injustice of this was not lost on Shyam Saran, India's Special

Envoy on Climate Change, who remarked; 'In India, I need to give electricity for light bulbs to half a billion [people]. In the West, you want to drive your Mercedes as fast as you want. We have "survival" emissions you have "lifestyle" emissions.' [35]

Even the language used to describe the phenomenon became a battleground. Partly due to pressure from the United States and major oil producers in the Middle East, the incendiary 'global warming' was gradually replaced by the more neutral-sounding 'climate change'.[36] However, the use of such euphemisms failed to douse the issue. Far from it; any unusual scientific phenomenon could find itself associated with climate change, even if the evidence and understanding was shaky. Environmentalists had long been raising concerns about the possibility that gorillas, tigers and orangutans would become extinct in the wild; now, suddenly, the threat came closer to home, as everyday species such as bees and thrushes began to suffer massive population falls. For many lay people, exotic animals in Africa or Asia were essentially abstractions (seen only on the National Geographic or Discovery Channel), but the idea that we might wake up one morning unaccompanied by birdsong suddenly felt far more real, and frightening.

Was the devastation of New Orleans by Hurricane Katrina in 2005 a sign of imminent global catastrophe? Were Cyclone Nargis and the Sichuan earthquake – which took place within days of one another in 2008 – directly related? Were humans entirely to blame for the bushfires that ravaged the Australian state of Victoria in February 2009, or were they merely lighting a naturally-primed touch paper? Even if responsibility for events such as these could not be conclusively pinned on man, they did remind us what a capricious monster Mother

Nature could be, and how ultimately feeble and presumptuous any notion of human achievement was when confronted with her wrath.

And it was not just climactic events that caused concern. Outbreaks of diseases such as H5N1 ('avian flu') and 'SARS' (Severe Acute Respiratory Syndrome) – both of which centred on Asia – raised the question of the extent to which personal freedoms might be curtailed in pursuit of maintaining public health. Countries such as Singapore (not a place renowned for its embrace of Western-style social liberalism) had no compunction about imposing screening and quarantine on people suspected of being infected. The threat of H1N1 ('swine flu') – which began in Mexico in 2009 – also brought to the fore the issue of uncontrolled migration, a hot-button topic in the recent US election.

As with any crisis, the cultural community was happy to show its support for the battle against global warming and climate change. But there was a problem here. When it came to the big moral causes of previous decades – AIDS, famine in Africa, war in Vietnam or Iraq – there was nothing inappropriate about staging a big rock festival, or even making a campaigning movie. It might seem ostentatious, but if it raised awareness and/or cash, surely that outweighed any negatives? However, global warming was different; environmental impact now had to be taken into consideration. A world tour by a successful rock band could generate thousands of tonnes of carbon dioxide,[37] while environmentally-themed Hollywood blockbusters, such as *The Day After Tomorrow* (2004), not only raised awareness of potential catastrophe but also contributed to its likelihood.

Efforts were made to minimize the impact of big productions and events. The Live Earth shows in 2007 were explicitly staged as eco-themed variants on 1985's Live Aid. The organizers made a point of staging the events in numerous locations, linked by TV and internet connections rather than transatlantic jet-setting. The producers of the campaigning film *The Age of Stupid* went even further, the 2009 London premiere being staged in a solar-powered cinema inside a tent in Leicester Square.

But such high-profile, one-off gestures were not enough. Of increasing environmental concern were plastic bags, which used environmentally-unfriendly fossil fuels in production, took years to decompose in landfill and caused the deaths of countless seabirds and other wildlife. In 2007, the designer Anya Hindmarch produced an environmentally-friendly shopping bag, conspicuously labelled 'I'm Not A Plastic Bag', which immediately became a must-have consumer item. Everywhere, retailers picked up on the idea, but it was hard to tell whether consumers really were changing their ways or were simply now amassing vast quantities of hessian (rather than plastic) bags. Other initiatives also had uncertain results. When supermarkets in Ireland started actively discouraging customers from using plastic bags there was a noticeable increase in the sales of bin liners; what the powers-that-be had failed to realize was that consumers were already in a recycling mindset, reusing unwanted supermarket bags to line their bins.

So, a serious question emerged. What impact was all this activity actually having on climate change? Earth Hour 2009, a shutdown of non-essential electric lights in over 80 countries for one hour in March 2009, certainly achieved plenty of coverage for the cause, but it was less clear what was practically achieved. And it was all well and good that Madonna, Kanye West and the Police took time out to tell us that global warming was a serious matter, or that Cormac

McCarthy's novel *The Road* [38] (2006) won the Pulitzer Prize for its depiction of a world destroyed by a non-specific environmental disaster, but this was not going to save the planet. Meanwhile, public discourse degenerated into a competition to declare how bad the environmental situation was, and how much worse it might conceivably get. At the same time, business and political leaders seemed slow to deliver firm initiatives that might remedy it. Meanwhile, the clocked ticked relentlessly towards Copenhagen, December 2009, where a new global deal on climate change was due to be agreed.

This gap between words and action was exemplified by the career of Al Gore, who had spent much of the decade raising awareness about the risks of global warming, most notably through his 2006 Oscar-winning documentary *An Inconvenient Truth*. Gore's efforts would see him earn a share of the Nobel Peace Prize in 2007. But Gore's worthy contribution came *after* he had been vice president of the United States for eight years, during which time he had surely been better placed to do something about the problem than he was as an unaligned activist and talking head. Gore could claim (with some justification) that his campaign was a form of redemption for the opportunities he had failed to take when he was in office, but did that really make things better?

To be fair, Gore was hardly alone. The political leaders of the major powers were in a hugely difficult situation. They understood that carbon emissions were wreaking havoc on the environment, but they were also responsible for the economic wellbeing of their countries and people, which meant business, technological progress, development, building, transport and spending – all of which inevitably led to carbon emissions. In the UK, hopes of a 'new green deal' –

whereby investment in natural infrastructure and green technologies such as wind, solar and geothermal would not only save the planet but also create valuable new 'green collar' jobs – seemed to wilt in the face of the 2008 credit crunch and cumbersome planning laws (although the government's 'Carbon Transition Plan', announced in July 2009, went some way towards addressing these issues). Meanwhile, vast amounts of government money were poured into failing financial institutions, to the consternation of environmentalists such as George Monbiot, who exclaimed; 'Do we want to be remembered as the generation that saved the banks and let the biosphere collapse?'[39]

By the end of the decade, only one country – the low-lying island nation the Maldives (which was at particular risk from rising Indian Ocean levels) – had announced serious plans to become carbon-neutral.[40] While this was undoubtedly welcome news, it was difficult to see how the efforts of a country of 385,000 people could have anything more than symbolic impact, especially when compared with the emissions of the US and developing countries.

Western governments, meanwhile, mustered a mixed response. The EU established the world's first large-scale emissions trading scheme, but critics complained it encouraged destructive development and merely lined the pockets of the rich. Targets for reduced emissions were set, but were accused of being watered down by corporate and national lobbying. Still, at least there was some movement, and recognition that there was a problem to solve. Over in the US, businesses started looking at developing technological solutions to climate change, encouraged no doubt by the words of Silicon Valley venture capitalist (and early backer of Google) John Doerr; 'Green technologies – going green – is bigger than the internet. It could be the biggest economic opportunity of the 21st century.'[41] Back in Europe, a giant solar power tower complex opened in the Spanish desert, 20 miles outside Seville.

Looking beyond the West, countries such as Qatar and Saudi Arabia (which had made their money from good old-fashioned oil) also turned their attention to new opportunities. Outside Abu Dhabi, a futuristic zero-carbon city and research park, Masdar, began to rise from the sands. Meanwhile, China, which for much of the decade had enjoyed impressive economic growth (but had not enjoyed being vilified for its impressive carbon emissions), revealed late in the decade that it was formulating a plan to provide a fifth of its energy needs from renewable sources by 2020, a target that would match that of the EU.

Despite the encouraging words of John Doerr and others, the US had been relatively slow off the mark when it came to tackling climate change. This was perhaps not surprising considering George W Bush's personal background in oil. Indeed, Bush's foreign policy had partly been defined by the need to guarantee supplies of the black stuff so that Americans would not have to slam the brakes on. In this context, Bush's support for drilling in the wilderness of Alaska made perfect economic sense; if the US could guarantee its own oil supplies, maybe there wouldn't need to be so many wars in the Middle East. Energy security and independence were key.

But even governments that supposedly aspired to left-of-centre ideologies – from the New Labour administration in Britain to the communist rulers of China – were desperate to encourage business, entrepreneurship and capitalism. Entire economies were based on the principle that people worked to earn money to pay for goods and services, and the more goods and services they paid for the better. If consumers were so concerned about the environmental impact of their purchases, well, they could always ask not to have them put in a plastic bag, thus taking away a pleasant feeling of worthiness along with their new CD or can of beans.

It was this idea – the moral perfection and fundamental necessity of capitalism – that had sustained Western democracies in their stand-off with communism until the early 1990s, and which had also offered a clear ideological distinction between 'the West' and 'the terrorists'. After every terrorist outrage, concerned politicians would be filmed walking in malls, main streets and high streets, encouraging a nervous populace to hit back at the bombers by doing what they loved best – going shopping. Conspicuous consumption was no longer just a pleasurable activity, it was a civic, democratic duty.[42]

And what could be wrong with that? The cash was there, and if it wasn't, there was always credit. Surely even global warming wasn't going to stop that?

# Chapter 4

# Keeping it real

'You should live every day like it's your birthday.'
Paris Hilton

**Jump the couch** (*verb*) to exhibit frenetic behaviour (2005)
**Celebutard** (*noun*) a stupid celebrity (2007)

For much of the Noughties, it was the medium rather than the message that grabbed the headlines. Music, news, gossip and art were still being widely generated and discussed, but they were being transmitted and received in ways unimaginable just a generation before.

The rapid expansion in broadband internet access meant that tapping into, storing and moving large quantities of data became increasingly easy – whether at home, work or on the move. This had greatest impact on the music industry (see Chapter 8), but television also got caught up in the excitement. With products such as the BBC's 'catch-up' service iPlayer, and Hulu (an online video-streaming site backed by Fox, NBC Universal and Disney), viewers had greater flexibility as to how, when and where they watched programmes – and this was only the legitimate side of the business.

In the early years of the decade, digital video recorders such as TiVo ('a VCR on steroids') had offered unprecedented control to TV viewers, while putting the fear of God into broadcasters by making it even easier to skip commercials.[43] Now 'torrents' technology enabled computer users to copy and share TV shows without permission or payment almost as easily as they could manipulate music files.

Apart from the stunning financial hit this inflicted on the industry, it effectively consigned the idea of television as a shared experience to a fuzzy, decidedly low-definition past. People in their 40s and beyond looked back fondly to the days when millions would sit down in front of the late night news or the final episode of M*A*S*H. Multi-channel TV, coupled with online playback, meant that the televisual water-cooler moment ('Did you see Seinfeld/Miami Vice/Casualty last night?') was increasingly restricted to live sports events. Meanwhile, widescreen and plasma TVs – seemingly designed to make viewing a communal event – instead became an emblem of conspicuous consumption; a new toy for the bachelor pad, to be enjoyed alone.

DVD came into its own in the Noughties, becoming the preferred format for watching movies at home. Further enhancements, such as Blu-Ray, remained niche purchases. Sales of DVD, particularly in the form of box sets, went some way towards bridging the advertising-shaped gap in the balance sheets of the TV industry; although this gap also reflected a lack of nerve among mainstream networks and channels. The gritty US cop series The Wire, for example, was one of the most critically acclaimed TV offerings of the decade, but its audience (and ad revenue) potential was hampered by the fact it was screened on the cable channel HBO. Meanwhile, in the UK, the show was screened on the obscure FX channel, struggling to approach audience figures of 100,000. The belated decision by the BBC to put the show out on terrestrial TV certainly increased its potential audience, but did nothing to secure advertising revenue.

Disseminated around the globe in various media, some shows that might normally have been ditched due to poor ratings lived on in DVD and cyberspace. Fans around the world could get together online to discuss plot, characterization, script-writing and special effects, or even to pressurize studios into further developing shows. Joss Whedon's superb space western TV series *Firefly*, cancelled in December 2002 due to poor ratings, was granted a full-length feature film release (*Serenity*, 2005) that gave existing fans closure and generated fresh box set sales from new fans that had never seen the original series. Like 'indie music', 'cult TV' achieved widespread success and exposure that brought into question its very identity. This phenomenon only increased as more shows were made available through video streaming and catch-up; a trend that threatened to overturn the dominance of the box set.

Despite the enhanced home-viewing experience offered by DVD and other formats, cinema receipts remained remarkably robust throughout the Noughties, especially for big-budget spectaculars such as 2008's *The Dark Knight*, which seemed cramped even on a 42-inch TV screen. This movie also saw Hollywood finally working out how to make best use of IMAX technology; never before had the skyscrapers of Hong Kong been able to induce such intense vertigo.

Technology also permeated the world of publishing, with varying results. Newspapers in particular seemed punch-drunk from the impact of online content, unsure whether to spurn or embrace the web. Giants such as the *New York*

*Times* appeared wrong-footed as attempts to make readers pay to read papers on screen had limited success; circulations began to fall away. After all, why should you pay for content when MSN, Google and freebie news sheets were feeding your data habit (even if there was a resulting drop in quality)? As the science journalist Ben Goldacre put it; 'Through our purchasing behaviour we have communicated to newspapers that we want them to be large and cheap more than we want them to be adequately researched.'[44] Content aside, the advent of free online advertising sites such as Craigslist and Gumtree inflicted grievous damage on the revenue model of print newspapers, especially local ones.

When the credit crunch finally hit in 2008 – provoking a massive downturn in advertising spend – a number of local papers went to the wall; even big nationals trembled under the threat of closure. Magazines, in particular lifestyle and entertainment titles, suffered similar fates – *Smash Hits*, *Arena* and *Blender* all disappeared from the shelves.[45] There were exceptions; *Vice* magazine (which launched in Canada back in 1994) flourished, mainly on the strength of its website and broadband TV service VBS. Outside lifestyle and entertainment, a few titles actually expanded; the tech magazine *Wired* successfully launching a UK version in April 2009. But the received wisdom by the end of the decade was that saving journalism (rather than saving print) was the priority.

Oddly, it was the world's oldest mass medium that appeared to suffer the fewest upheavals. Print-on-demand and electronic page make-up technology took book production out of the exclusive control of publishers (and into the hands of authors), while electronic reading devices such as Amazon's Kindle finally gave us the paperless book. In Japan, a new phenomenon – the '*keitai shousetsu*' (or 'cell phone novel') – made its mark.

Written to be read on the small screen of a mobile, language was concise and simple, the subject matter usually romance. Late in the decade, Penguin New York announced that it had commissioned a new volume – *Twitterature* – containing some of the jewels of Western literature in 20 'tweets' (sentences comprising no more than 140 characters, as per micro-blogging site Twitter protocol) or fewer. James Joyce anyone?

Still, suggestions that these were the most important developments in reading since Gutenberg and the invention of moving type seemed premature. Publishers still published books (with paper pages and cardboard covers) and readers still wanted to read them; indeed, many *keitai* novels later made it into conventional print. As for electronic devices such as the Kindle and Sony Reader, these might have been great for loading up titles for holiday, but it seemed many people still liked owning the offline versions, at least for the moment.

Nonetheless, online could not be ignored, even if you weren't officially in the book business. In an audacious move, Google, the US-based search engine giant, started offering online access to millions of books via its Google Book Search service. Subject to intense criticism from established publishers for alleged violations of intellectual property right, in October 2008 Google finally came to a revenue-sharing agreement with the industry.

As for the content of books, this increasingly seemed to be dictated by what had sold well in the past, publishers and agents desperately following trends rather than setting them. Not that these trends were anything new. So-called 'chick lit' titles – fiction centering on young single women whose lives revolve around men and shopping – were essentially an update of Jane Austen, while 'misery memoirs' – nonfiction centering on individuals surviving abuse and privation – were pretty much a rerun of *Oliver Twist*, without the social commentary. The misery memoirs, of course, had to be rooted in fact. This created embarrassment when it turned out that some publishers had been so keen to jump on board the misery bandwagon they had failed to exercise due diligence over the precise details of their authors' experience of abuse/ drugs/prostitution/prison (delete as appropriate).

Celebrity memoirs were another popular stream, continuing to attract massive advances for their authors throughout most of the Noughties. It seemed that as soon as someone had slept with a footballer or been evicted from a TV show there was a publisher waiting to turn the experience into a hardback; not the easiest of tasks when the subject was often still a teenager, although a nod to the misery market (poverty-stricken childhood, mental disorder etc) always helped. The logical progression from these content-light tomes was celebrity fiction, although the direct involvement of celebrities such as Pamela Anderson and Katie 'Jordan' Price in the books that bore their names was sometimes questionable.

However, not all successful books were such blatant attempts to appeal to the lowest common denominator. Popular science remained a thriving genre, and there was a boom in social science titles, applying techniques of economics and sociology to everyday situations. Malcolm Gladwell's *The Tipping Point* (2000) and *Blink* (2005), and *Freakonomics* (2005) by Steven Levitt and Stephen Dubner, created a new genre somewhere between science, business and self-help – and there were plenty of others delighted to hitch a ride on their coat-tails.

The closing years of the decade saw a similar slew of books about religion, prompted by mainstream polemical tracts from atheists such as Richard Dawkins and Christopher Hitchens. Meanwhile – particularly in the United States – the bookshelves groaned under the weight of political tomes, many of which seemed to be written entirely in capital letters. Notable culprits included Michael Moore and Al Franken from the left, and Ann Coulter and Bill O'Reilly from the right. A less bellicose tome entitled *The Audacity of Hope* (2006), written by a relatively unknown senator from Illinois, became, like its author Barack Obama, a global sensation.

As well as politics, the average reader also seemed to have a healthy appetite for knowledge. In the UK, unexpected successes included Lynne Truss' *Eats Shoots & Leaves* (a guide to the correct use of punctuation, published in 2003) and the *Schott's Miscellany* series, seemingly random collections of weird and wonderful facts. *The Book of General Ignorance* (2006) did well on both sides of the Atlantic. These, and the popularity of novels such as *Starter for Ten* (2003) and *Q & A* (2005) – both of which were subsequently adapted as movies, the latter as the Oscar-bedecked *Slumdog Millionaire* (2008) – may have been partly inspired by the popularity of high-prize TV quiz shows throughout the decade. However, the parallel notoriety of Pierre Bayard's *How To Talk About Books You Haven't Read* (2007) suggested that the desire for learning was perhaps somewhat shallower than it first appeared.

Taking a lead from the web, reading became a more interactive, social activity. Online and offline book groups flourished, providing an accessible, non-threatening forum for debate. Titles such as *The Shadow of the Wind*, first published (in English) in 2004, and *The Kite Runner* (2003) achieved word-of-mouth success from this process. The book club phenomenon was taken up and amplified by television; a recommendation from the likes of Oprah Winfrey in the US or Richard and

Judy in the UK could work miracles for a new title, as well as resurrecting in the popular imagination such classics as *Anna Karenina*. Jonathan Franzen, author of *The Corrections* (2001), created a storm of publicity of his own when he expressed unease about appearing on Oprah's list; James Frey created an even bigger one when he tearfully admitted that his 2003 drug memoir, *A Million Little Pieces,* drifted rather closer to the shores of fiction than he'd suggested.

In the Noughties, books were newsworthy, and talkworthy. Literary shindigs, such as the UK's Hay festival, raised their profile as they continued to offer an eclectic range of talks, debates, music and film to a funky (if somewhat middle class) cross-section of the community. As the artist Dinos Chapman noted; 'It's like everyone has gone to Glastonbury and parked their parents there.' Virtual author tours also gathered momentum.

Still, the biggest story of the decade was undoubtedly the *Harry Potter* fantasy series. JK Rowling's tales of the bespectacled schoolboy wizard created a level of devotion that drew comparisons with Dickens; fans regularly camping outside bookshops in anticipation of the midnight release of the latest instalment. Even if some critics sniffed at Rowling's verbose prose style (each successive volume seeming to be twice the length of the previous one), she clearly knew how to reach out to reluctant readers and listeners of all ages. The books sold in their millions (as likely through online retailers such as Amazon as through conventional, bricks-and-mortar bookshops), as did the CD versions. Teen (and pre-teen) books raised their profile, with authors such as Philip Pullman and Eoin Colfer coming to the fore.

If critics were lukewarm about Rowling and Potter, they were positively heated about another bestseller. Dan Brown's *The*

*Da Vinci Code* (2003) was essentially an old-fashioned airport novel, with pretensions to academic authority that made its flimsy plot seem even more preposterous. But the book – with its clunky prose and predictable characters – sold in vast quantities, in dozens of different languages, and spawned a legion of copycats and commentaries. Thousands of fans made a pilgrimage to the Louvre to retrace its action.

Although *The Da Vinci Code* wasn't overtly a political book, there was something about it that seemed to capture the Noughties' sense of fear and paranoia; the sense that things were not quite as they ought to be. In cinema, this odd mixture of escapism and neurosis was best exemplified by the Wachowski brothers' *Matrix* films, the second and third instalments of which appeared in 2003. The idea that what we perceive to be reality is a glossy delusion crafted by our political and economic masters was not new (the French theorist Jean Baudrillard had been exploring this possibility for decades), but it did tap into a mood of increased scepticism about the veracity of the mass media – especially in the wake of 9/11 and the various adventures that followed therefrom.

The *Matrix* films also gave renewed impetus to sequels. Successful movies – often derived from pre-existing entertainment products (for example the *Pirates of the Caribbean* franchise, which was based on a Disney theme-park ride) – were squeezed dry as producers attempted to reproduce their success. It may have made financial sense, but the law of diminishing returns usually kicked in; the word 'threequel' defining a third instalment of a series in which part two had already come perilously close to shark-jumping. A rare exception was the *Lord of the Rings* franchise, in which the final part grabbed the Best Picture Oscar that had eluded its predecessors. Indeed, the Noughties saw a number of respected artists gaining a 'better late than never' Oscar. The fact that Martin Scorsese and Kate Winslet were not being rewarded for their finest work was diplomatically overlooked.

Cinema wasn't all about bells-and-whistles blockbusters of course. Documentaries, especially films with a distinct point of view, made it to the multiplexes. Michael Moore's *Fahrenheit 9/11* (2004) became the most successful documentary of all time, raking in over $200m worldwide. Moore returned in 2007 with *Sicko*, about the American healthcare system. From the other side of the ideology wars (although using the same weapon), *Michael Moore Hates America* (2004) turned its fire on the vociferous liberal, while *Expelled* (2008) attempted to discredit Darwinian theories of evolution. Not all documentaries were so polemical however. The French-made *March of the Penguins* (2005) based its success on the inherent comedy and pathos of its subjects (although some American religious and political activists saw it as a parable for the wonders of monogamy and traditional family values), while *Man on Wire*, the 2009 Oscar winner for Best Documentary Feature, was a celebration of individual expression rather than dogma – Philippe Petit cavorting between the Twin Towers of the World Trade Center, obliquely reminding us of a time when they were just tall buildings.

But in mainstream dramatic film-making there was less originality. Hollywood seemed content to raid children's favourites, such as the Narnia chronicles, or to resurrect comic-book superheroes. The latter had varying degrees of success; Batman earned a new lease of life, the Incredible Hulk just made critics and movie-goers angry, twice. Of course, independent and low-budget film-makers (and those operating outside the English-speaking world) felt less need to produce safe, bankable hits; movies such as *Irréversible* (2002), *9 Songs* (2004) and *Antichrist* (2009) pushing the boundaries of what was acceptable in their depictions of sex and violence.

An interesting trend emerged of independently-minded film-makers working with mainstream studios and distributors. The commercial and critical impact of Quentin Tarantino in the 1990s had convinced investors that it was possible to reach accommodation with creative mavericks. Although Tarantino didn't manage to replicate his own earlier success in the Noughties, quirky, low-budget movies such as *Sideways* (2004), *Little Miss Sunshine* (2006) and *Juno* (2007) offered a respite from orcs and wizards, without getting too overtly 'arthouse'.

Despite predictions of its demise, intelligent, compelling television programming also continued to be produced, especially in the US (most notably from cable TV channel HBO). *The Sopranos* and *The Wire* created big, complex tableaux that drew comparisons with Dickens, Balzac, Dostoyevsky and Hardy, while *The West Wing* effectively created an alternative American administration – one in which people spoke in coherent sentences. In the UK, the regenerated *Dr Who* was a critical and ratings triumph, one of the few shows that seemed able to revive that lost social phenomenon, family viewing.

*Dr Who* offered escapism, taking more than a few pointers from US hits such as *Buffy the Vampire Slayer* and its spin-off *Angel*.[46] But television also tapped into a feeling of entrapment – *24*, *Alias*, *Heroes* and the British-made dramas *State of Play* (later adapted as a Hollywood movie) and *Spooks* (titled *MI-5* in the US) all presented a world populated by liars, traitors and conspirators; a scenario that resonated widely with viewers. The desert-island smash *Lost*, meanwhile, emulated the 1960s classic *The Prisoner* in that its primary purpose seemed to be to get viewers to argue about what the heck was going on.

Big, often prestigious, drama productions earned plaudits and respectable viewing figures, but they are far from telling the whole story of television in the Noughties. As TV's market share was progressively eroded by online and virtual media, broadcasters and producers sought new ways for viewers to become part of the experience, as they were with social networks and video games. The talent show – a tried and tested format whereby 'ordinary people' vied for fame and fortune – seemed an obvious vehicle, and the Noughties saw the genre reach new heights. Originating in (of all places) New Zealand, the format of the 1999 series *Popstars* was taken up by broadcasters around the world, reaching the shores of Britain in late 2000, where it spawned the fractious quintet Hear'Say and then (rather more successfully) Girls Aloud. The essential difference between *Popstars* and old-style talent shows was that developments in technology now meant that each vote cast by a viewer added cash to the bottom line. For broadcasters haemorrhaging valuable advertising revenue to new media, the attraction was obvious.

The format seemingly knew no bounds, spawning the hugely successful 'Idol' and 'Got Talent' franchises, and making the sardonic Simon Cowell a household name. Inevitably, the vast majority of performers were doomed to oblivion; even winners tended to enjoy only a brief flurry of success, their lasting contribution to the cult of celebrity being as the answer to a pub quiz question. The likes of Girls Aloud, Will Young, Kelly Clarkson and Leona Lewis were rare exceptions.

It is quite possible, of course, that talented performers such as Clarkson and Lewis might have made it to stardom without the assistance of Simon Cowell. This cannot be said, however, for the celebrities launched by another successful strand of Noughties programming, known without any apparent sense of irony as 'reality TV'.

Like the talent shows, there was nothing particularly new about this format. Michael Apted's *Up* series of documentaries – following a group of Britons from childhood through adulthood – had begun way back in 1964, while *An American Family* (1973) and *The Family* (a British series from 1974) had used fly-on-the-wall camera techniques that raised issues around the effect of constant surveillance. Meanwhile, the 1990s saw MTV's *The Real World* (a show which followed the fortunes of a group of young housemates, each season moving to a different city) and the student-based *The Living Soap* from the BBC. But nothing quite prepared us for the show that essentially summed up not just television in the Noughties but also a significant slice of popular culture.

Like *Popstars*, *Big Brother* had unlikely beginnings, this time in the Netherlands. By the year 2000, it was being broadcast in both the UK and the US. The British version, first broadcast on Channel 4, achieved respectable but not startling viewing figures until one of the housemates (immediately dubbed 'Nasty Nick' by the tabloids) was discovered to be plotting against the others. In retrospect, this was the moment that set the agenda for celebrity culture throughout the decade; a modern reimagining of the serpent in Eden, Nick destroyed the notion that 'ordinary people' on TV should be innocent or lack self-awareness. The contestants on the first series of *Big Brother* seemed to be on the show out of a sense of curiosity; from series two onwards, they wanted to be famous.

The success of *Big Brother* affected other reality sub-genres. The various talent shows became less about raw ability, more about the back stories of the competitors – a contestant who had been bullied at school or who suffered from some kind of disability might guarantee a surge of support that made their ability to hit the high notes irrelevant. The global fame of Susan Boyle, a contestant on the 2009 series of *Britain's Got Talent*, was partly down to the stunning realization that somebody so clearly outside the celebrity loop might be able to do something better than someone we'd heard of.

Faced with competition from this instant fame machine, 'real' celebrities (the soap stars, pop singers, models and footballers who had previously dominated the chat shows and gossip columns) fought back. If *Big Brother* turned ordinary people into celebrities, shows such as *I'm a Celebrity...Get Me Out of Here!* forced the famous to expose their human foibles. Later, their abilities to dance, cook, skate, even conduct an orchestra, were held up to public scrutiny.

Pretty soon, the boundaries between 'deserved' and 'manu-factured' celebrity were irrevocably blurred. Lionel Richie's daughter Nicole parlayed her friendship with Paris Hilton into a full-blown career, while Bruce Jenner suddenly discovered that he was less legendary Olympic athlete, more Kim Kardashian's step-dad. Even sports stars who retained a career in the stadium or on the pitch found themselves transformed into 'brands', most notably the England footballer David Beckham.

The rarefied world of the visual arts also became obsessed with celebrity to an extent not seen since the heyday of Andy Warhol. When, in September 2008 (as the world economy reeled from the collapse of Lehman Brothers), Damien Hirst auctioned the contents of his *Beautiful Inside My Head Forever* exhibition for an astonishing £111m, were the punters buying the art or a vicarious slice of the artist? One way or another, 20 years after the staging of his groundbreaking warehouse show *Freeze* (within a year of 1987's Black Monday), the now not-so-Young British Artist Hirst had beaten the system once again. Meanwhile, another artist, the anti-celebrity Banksy, continued to attract huge sums for his street art, despite (or because of) the fact no one really knew who he was.

Of course, celebrity could go horribly wrong. The degeneration of Britney Spears from pop moppet to rock bottom was a very public cautionary tale for this very public decade, as was the meltdown of Susan Boyle – going from frumpish obscurity to *Britain's Got Talent*, *Oprah* and a psychiatric hospital in a matter of weeks; a terrifyingly fast trajectory, even by the standards of reality TV. The disintegration of Michael Jackson was even more distressing, particularly as he truly possessed outrageous talent. His death in 2009 provoked worldwide mourning (and a profoundly strange televised memorial service), but in truth Jackson the man had died years before, to be replaced by a grotesque post-human, a parody of celebrity concocted by a cabal of publicists and plastic surgeons.

Still, there were two women in the Noughties who exemplified and transcended the whole concept of celebrity – one, an American, apparently treating the whole experience as some sort of hyperreal situation comedy; the other, a Briton, lurching from farce into tragedy.

Paris Hilton was born to be a particular kind of celebrity – a trust-fund model, she was the sort of girl who naturally finds herself gracing yachts in the south of France and red carpets on Hollywood Boulevard. But, in the middle of the Noughties, Paris made the leap from socialite to global brand, becoming (in the words of pop star Lady Gaga) 'Mrs Fame'. Paris' appearance on a reality show called *The Simple Life* coincided with the leakage of footage that showed her administering intimate gratification to a gentleman friend – something that might have derailed her fledgling career in earlier times, but which now just added another fascination to her manu-factured Noughties identity. In quick succession we had Paris the pop star,[47] Paris the author, Paris the actress, Paris the tongue-in-cheek politician; even, after a succession of driving violations, Paris the celebrity jailbird (and, in conjunction with that, Paris the born-again Christian). Throughout her travails, Paris (mostly) managed to maintain her trademark lopsided smile, suggesting that she was nowhere near as stupid as her brand identity suggested.

Jade Goody never claimed to be clever, although it is just possible her entire life and career comprised some sort of elaborate, Andy Kaufman-style piece of conceptual perfor-mance. Initially just another *Big Brother* contestant – and not even a winner at that – Jade was loud, raucous and apparently woefully ignorant; qualities that made her an easy target for the tabloid press.

But, unlike the other housemates, Jade Goody's moment of fame extended well beyond its allotted mayfly lifespan. Her back story (born poor in one of the less salubrious corners of south London) smacked of the misery memoir, but her rise to fame symbolized the vicarious wish-fulfilment that was at the heart of Noughties celebrity culture. If Jade Goody could become a media fixture, surely anyone could? She didn't need to do anything; she just *was*. At the launch of her perfume, Shh...Jade Goody, the budding star declared; 'People think they'll smell like Jade Goody. But you're not having my BO or my foot smell or anything like that. You're not actually going to smell like me. There's no parts of me in it.'

Such ingenuous dimness sustained Jade's career until early 2007. Jade (along with her mother and boyfriend) was now deemed famous enough to take part in the 'celebrity' variant of *Big Brother*, during which she became involved in racially-charged slanging matches with the Bollywood actress Shilpa Shetty.[48] Suddenly she was (in)famous *for* something.

Under the guidance of the publicist Max Clifford, Jade attempted to redeem her tarnished celebrity, culminating in a third *Big Brother* appearance, this time on the Indian version of the show, in 2008. It was here that she discovered she was suffering from cervical cancer. Reality show contestants had faced up to their mortality before, but the terminal illnesses of contestants on MTV's *The Real World* were part of the package; Pedro Zamora and Frankie Abernethy were selected in part because they were ill. Jade's illness wasn't part of the script; it was a genetic improvisation, beyond the control of the most ruthless TV executive.

The merciless progress of the disease was followed in grim detail by the press, camera crews camped outside the Royal Marsden hospital on London's Fulham Road. Others had more privileged access to the celebrity patient, who was keen to earn enough money to secure her children's future. Originally a UK phenomenon, towards the end Jade's story was taken up by the global media;[49] she even received a telephone message of support from Michael Jackson (a man who had led even more of his life in the spotlight than Jade).

Jade Goody died in the early hours of Mother's Day 2009 at the age of just 27. If she had had the strength, she could have leafed through the black-edged memorial edition of her life *OK!* magazine already had on the shelves. The day after Jade actually died, the *Sun* newspaper devoted its first 10 pages, plus a 16-page supplement, to her. More than one distraught fan compared her to Princess Diana, and the temporary mood of emotional derangement was certainly similar (and will, presumably, provoke similar revisionist denial among the participants in years to come). Fittingly, just a month after her death, plans were announced for Jade Goody, the musical.

Jade Goody's life and death summed up the paradox of Noughties celebrity culture; successful celebrities had to be at once real, unreal and hyperreal; consumers of the product had to admire them as if they were secular deities and yet at the same time believe they might bump into them in the laundrette. Jade Goody offered the right combination because her special quality was her own exceptional mediocrity. There are thousands like her in the Western world, and we barely notice them.

It was not Jade herself who exemplified (in the words of broadcaster Michael Parkinson) 'all that is paltry and wretched about Britain today',[50] it was the bizarre media circus of the decade that allowed her to flourish. It was this same circus, however, that enabled the call to lower the age for cervical smears in England to be heard at the highest level, a public-service corollary that supposedly justified the saturation coverage of Jade's decline. Reality was acting as an alibi for the excesses of the unreal.

# Chapter 5
# Keeping it unreal

'And if any number can be said
to encapsulate our times, 404 is it.'
Michael Bywater, *Lost Worlds*[51]

**Pwn** (*verb*) to defeat or best another person, usually in an
online context (2006)

According to the comedian Robin Williams, if you can remember the 60s you probably weren't there. In the Noughties,
it could be argued, if you were entirely there then you probably
weren't there either. Like the Hollywood musicals of the
1930s, many entertainment products projected an alternative
reality, encouraging people to leave their troubles at the door,
if only for the duration of the show.

But the Noughties was the decade when virtual reality – once the
preserve of sci-fi books (eg Ben Bova's 1969 novel *The Dueling
Machine*) or movies (eg Steven Lisberger's 1982 film *Tron*) –
could be summoned up with little more effort than it took to
order a pizza. The launch of Second Life in 2003 allowed users
to create alternative identities (avatars) within an alternative
online environment. Bands, comedians and theatre groups

staged performances in this new 3D world, while global brands such as Sony, Reuters, Ikea and IBM opened for business. But there was an air of self-conscious irony about this corporate involvement. While everyone knew that Second Life wasn't 'real', to say so explicitly marked you out as a killjoy. Inevitably, much of the corporate positioning in the virtual world felt more like a desperate attempt to appear cool; once established in Second Life, many brands didn't quite know what to do with themselves. Reuters' reporter quit in 2008.

Individuals, however, were more confident in virtuality; their problems came when they returned to reality. More than one online love affair between perfect avatars crashed in flames when their less-than-perfect physical versions made themselves known.[52] That said, some corporates did make a success of their virtual involvement; for example, the Swedish chain H&M joined forces with Electronic Arts to create a 'fashion pack' add-on to the hugely popular *Sims* game which contained virtual replicas of real-world H&M clothing, as well as the resources to recreate a store online. Meanwhile, the economist Edward Castronova calculated that if the virtual world Norrath (in Sony's game *EverQuest*) were translated to reality, it would boast a GNP of $2,266 per person, just behind that of Russia.[53]

Second Life was a fusion of two key areas of consumer technology that prospered in the Noughties – video games and social networking. Video games had changed out of all recognition from the pioneering days of *Pong* and *Tetris*. As with the internet, what was once seen as the territory of nerds, geeks or maladjusted teenage boys had morphed into a multi-billion-dollar industry to rival (and even outstrip) movies and music. Once again, the lines between different media blurred; games such as *Tomb Raider* became movies, while bands jostled to have their music featured in successful games. Even the Beatles, who had eschewed iTunes and Spotify, realized the potential of the gaming medium, launching the MTV-supported *Beatles: Rock Band* project in 2009. With *Rock Band*, gamers could let it be at the Cavern Club or get back to the Apple company roof in London's Savile Row.

The line between reality and virtuality also blurred. When the Maldives opened a virtual embassy in Second Life it provoked plenty of column inches in the real world, boosting the visibility of the small island nation as a tourist destination (which was, of course, the whole point).

Increasingly, as with the Jade Goody saga (see Chapter 4), it seemed that reality could only get a look in by hitching a ride on the back of its own digital shadow.

The beginning of the Noughties saw the launch of two groundbreaking consoles – Sony's PlayStation 2 in 2000 and Microsoft's Xbox (the software giant's first foray into gaming hardware) in 2001. At around the same time, a Cambrian explosion in broadband availability made it possible to play increasingly sophisticated games online from your PC or laptop.

Spotting the popularity of multi-player online games such as *World of Warcraft* and *Ragnarok*, Sony and Microsoft offered enhanced internet connectivity with subsequent versions of their consoles, making gaming a genuinely social activity. Meanwhile, products such as the hugely successful Nintendo Wii (which allowed the user to control the game with physical gestures as well as button presses) reintroduced us to the delights of singing, tennis and aerobics – activities we'd probably only abandoned because we'd got into video games. Not to be outdone, in June 2009 Microsoft unveiled its revolutionary 'Project Natal' hands-free control system, threatening to turn the gaming world on its head yet again.

As multi-player games such as *World of Warcraft* had allowed us to interact with other 'virtual' players, so in the Noughties it became perfectly acceptable to define people as 'friends' even though we'd never physically met them; in many cases, we didn't even know their real names. (This wasn't entirely a new phenomenon; the 1995 movie *Denise Calls Up*, directed by Hal Salwen, was about a group of 'friends' who communicated entirely by phone and fax because they were too busy to meet in person. In the following decade, only the preferred medium changed.)

This kind of virtual connection was a key component of social networking, which was itself central to the most significant technological phenomenon of the decade – Web 2.0. Web 2.0 was effectively the second coming (or second chance) of web development, following the spectacular bursting of the dotcom bubble in 2000/2001 (which marked the end of Web 1.0). Unfortunately, the thorny problem that had precipitated the dotcom crash – the difficulty of turning online innovations into cash ('monetizing') – was still not fully resolved. But, by 2004, a number of new products had emerged that would not only fundamentally change our relationship with technology but also our relationship with other media and, potentially, each other.

One of the first Web 1.0 phenomena to have seized the public imagination was the search engine, and this function stayed at the heart of later developments; the verb 'to Google'[54] becoming synonymous with looking something up on the web. With Google, the user entered certain key words and was returned a list of ranked web pages; the web page with the most/most important links appearing first. Beyond general search, some of the earliest Web 2.0 successes focused on providing answers to certain frequently asked questions, such as whatever happened to that kid you were at school with. Sites such as ClassMates and Friends Reunited sought to address this nostalgic yearning in a structured way; and it wasn't a huge conceptual leap from tracking down your old friends to making new ones, which was the original intent of Friendster. Later in the decade, sites such as WolframAlpha attempted to refine the process by providing specific answers to specific queries, while Microsoft launched its 'decision engine' Bing, which promised to bring the user more practically relevant and useful results. Both these developments hoped to better the Google search experience and challenge the company's undoubted dominance in the field.

Of course, search was not the only game in town. Social networking sites such as MySpace and Facebook meant that anyone who was vaguely computer literate was able to create a personalized presence on the web; there was no need to master complex coding or design tools. Once established online, users could interact with friends and strangers alike, or simply use their virtual home as a base to explore their own creativity – posting words, sounds and images to create an accurate or fabricated online identity. On MySpace, groups or solo artists could create a profile showcasing their music, which is how artists such as Lily Allen came to notice. This was also possible on Bebo, which had a similar facility for authors.

Everywhere you looked, social networking sites were gaining momentum, often outflanking the more established competition. Again, the ranked list of web pages returned by Google search was sometimes felt to be lacking; when users sought advice online for everyday, personal decisions, the word of friends and acquaintances (accessed via social networking sites) was generally considered more intimate and trustworthy. Of course, if you were worried, you could always buy up the newcomers, as Rupert Murdoch's powerful News Corporation had done with MySpace in July 2005, only to see Facebook pull ahead of its new baby.[55]

Meanwhile, out in the blogosphere, platforms such as Blogger and WordPress were starting to transform the media landscape. With the means of production no longer concentrated in the hands of a few big media companies, blogs began to proliferate, just as independent print fanzines had done in the slipstream of punk in the 1970s and 80s. Blogs allowed unprecedented freedom; the views of an amateur blogger in Argentina or Zambia no more or less accessible to the interested surfer than those of a professional commentator attached to the *New York Times* or *Sydney Morning Herald*.

But all this created a problem for the proprietors of news-papers, magazines and (increasingly) TV and radio stations, who no longer had a monopoly on gathering and interpreting data. The ethos of the web itself didn't help matters. Originally conceived as an 'open' platform – where information was freely exchangeable – the web resisted attempts at creating 'walled gardens', where access was privileged and/or chargeable (Rupert Murdoch's *Wall Street Journal* a notable exception to this rule). Behind this lurked a seemingly more substantive rationale – as web pundit Jeff Jarvis put it; 'Charging for content reduces audience, which in turn reduces advertising revenue. And putting a wall around content keeps it out of the conversation and devalues brands.' In May 2009, Rupert Murdoch called the dominant free-access model 'malfunctioning' and signalled a desire to extend online charging to his other newpapers;[56]

nonetheless, the web remained essentially an information free-for-all.

For established media companies – used to both controlling and charging for content – this not only spelt potential disaster for the bottom line but also for 'proper' journalism and journalists. Old-style hacks felt so threatened by the competition Web 2.0 presented that they judged it by the standards of their own trade rather than by its own paradigms. Journalists couldn't get their heads around the fact that blog posts were usually displayed in reverse chronological order;[57] because newspaper journalists didn't do that, bloggers must by definition be bad journalists. When the micro-blogging site Twitter (which allowed users to send messages containing no more than 140 characters) suddenly found critical mass in 2009, columnists took delight in highlighting the isolated inanity of minor celebrities announcing what they were having for dinner, which rather missed the point. The power of Twitter (and of blogs) lay not in individual posts but in the interaction between those posts and the posters. To compare the complaint of Stephen Fry stuck in a lift with a first-person report from Iraq is not even like comparing apples with oranges; it's like comparing apples with hang-gliding, or Trotskyism.

Moreover, Web 2.0 really came into its own when its various aspects joined up; for example, a band putting MP3s on MySpace or a YouTube clip embedded in a blog. As I type these words, I've just received a tweet from one Xan Phillips, someone I've never met; 'After Sam Johnston's comment on Facebook, I'm listening to "Telephone Call from Istanbul" by Tom Waits on Spotify and telling you on Twitter!' Despite early fears, bloggers and MySpacers were far from solipsistic cranks. Indeed, phenomena such as social networking simply could not exist in a vacuum; after all, as the founder of Facebook

Mark Zuckerberg reminded us, the original purpose of his site was 'to help people make sense of what's around them'.[58]

Again, the medium as well as the message defined the time and place. The most resonant images of 9/11 were largely the work of professional cameramen, but the London attacks of 2005 were defined by amateur camera-phone footage. Details of the November 2008 Mumbai attacks were relayed by Twitter, as were news and images of the airliner that crash-landed on the Hudson River in January 2009. In this new Web 2.0 world, if you could watch you could record, if you could speak you could broadcast, and if you could write you could publish. You could also do it remarkably quickly, Twitter disseminating news far faster than other services. No wonder Google got twitchy.

Still, to identify the tipping point for citizen journalism, we need to travel back a little further, to December 2004, when a powerful tsunami devastated the coasts of countries from Thailand to Tanzania. With digital still and/or video cameras and camera phones widespread among the many tourists present, ordinary people shared with professional journalists the ability to reach a wide audience — to show the world what they had seen and experienced. While the rise of citizen journalism perturbed many conventional media organizations, some were brave enough to embrace it, BBC News Online posting eye-witness accounts from individuals affected by the tsunami as well as videos and photos taken by survivors.

The new media were becoming increasingly relevant, and influential. In April 2009, Twitter was used to arrange a 'flash mob' demonstration against election-rigging in Moldova (forcing a recount), and in June 2009 to spread news of the post-election protests in Iran (at a time when foreign journalists were operating under increasingly severe restrictions). In April 2009, AudioBoo (the audio-blogging platform and iPhone app) recorded and disseminated sound bites from the G20 summit demonstrations in London. Meanwhile, the collaborative news site Digg – on which users could submit and vote for their favourite stories – continued to thrive. Conventional news and entertainment media had to get involved, or turn their faces to the wall and die. So journalists started blogging and reporters started tweeting, which may have been a wry comment on declining attention spans. That said, the Iranian situation demonstrated that, in a repressive climate, it was apparently simple technology such as Twitter that had the resilience and adaptability to make a difference. As the Harvard academic Jonathan Zittrain remarked; 'It is easy for Twitter feeds to be echoed everywhere else in the world. The qualities that make Twitter seem inane and half-baked are what make it so powerful.'[59]

For some, the arrival of the big boys in the blogosphere meant that it had become irretrievably tainted by commercialism. There was concern that 'the blogosphere, once a freshwater oasis of folksy self-expression and clever thought [had been] flooded by a tsunami of paid bilge'.[60] So celebrities who aspired to keep up with the times turned their attentions to Twitter. The first account to accrue 1 million followers was not that of a news organization or a web guru, but of the artfully goofy movie star Ashton Kutcher, whose 15 minutes of digital fame came when he posted a picture of his wife, actor Demi Moore, in her underwear.

Such crassness played into the hands of Web 2.0's critics, who saw in open-access projects such as Wikipedia something akin to the death of truth itself. As the Silicon Valley insider Andrew Keen commented; 'The professional is being replaced by the amateur, the lexicographer by the lay person, the Harvard professor by the unschooled populace.'[61] The notion of 'dumbing down' was on everybody's lips and on everybody's minds; exams were getting easier, television was getting stupider and nobody knew how to spell any more (despite the renewed popularity of spelling bees). To be fair, though, Wikipedia could hardly be held responsible for this perceived lack of expertise; indeed, the fact that its 'articles' were constantly revised, updated and checked meant that errors could be spotted and remedied much faster ('wiki', after all, is Hawaiian for quick) than they could in the old-style media to which old-school elitists like Keen were so committed. Accuracy on Wikipedia was generally high.

But what was wrong with amateurism anyway? Looking back to the pre-Wiki utopia of the 19th century, we find that James Murray and Henry Bradley – the two most important figures in the success of the greatest reference work of all, the *Oxford English Dictionary* – were largely self-taught philologists, and neither had been to university. Keen's complaints simply echoed those of the 15th-century Italian humanist Hieronimo Squarciafico, who had worried that the advent of Gutenberg's printed books would make people stupid.[62] Whatever the rights and wrongs of the situation, users voted with their mouse and their wallet. In March 2009, Microsoft announced that it was discontinuing its (disc and online) Encarta encyclopedia products, noting wryly 'people today seek and consume information in considerably different ways than in past years'. Wiki had eaten Bill Gates' lunch.

Viewed in the round, Web 2.0 could be seen as the manifestation of a general desire for self-expression and self-determination. In Western democracies, people were increasingly cynical about conventional political processes, seeing their rulers as opportunists – differentiated only by the particular brand of consumer capitalism they were peddling.

New technology offered a means for individuals to make their voices heard; it may not have been any more effective than putting a cross next to the name of some guy in a suit every four or five years, but it was certainly more immediate, and it was definitely more fun. And it wasn't just online that such involvement increased. In the summer of 2009, the sculptor Antony Gormley gave randomly chosen individuals the chance to make an exhibition of themselves on the fourth plinth in London's Trafalgar Square. This new mood of inclusiveness was summed up in the title of movie-maker Michel Gondry's 2008 memoir, *You'll Like This Film Because You're In It*.

Of course, the desire for fame and recognition, however fleeting, had its downside. In 2008, psychiatrists identified 'Truman Show syndrome' (a reference to the 1998 film starring Jim Carrey), sufferers of which believed they were participants in a reality TV show.

Where elitists such as Keen did have a point was that self-appointed pundits, such as Wikipedia contributors and the people who posted reviews on Amazon, relied to a greater or lesser extent on the more traditional media for their base content. If the worst happened, and newspapers were made obsolete by unverifiable online content, the 'unschooled populace' would suddenly realize that they had nothing to comment upon. Bloggers and their ilk were parasites, inadvertently killing their host. Meanwhile, that host was sometimes complicit in its own fate. In April 2009, Twitter saw a 43% rise in traffic when Oprah Winfrey sent a tweet on her TV show.

But in some ways the relationship between pundit and press was symbiotic rather than parasitic. Indolent journalists were quite happy to extrapolate an entire salacious article from a celebrity's Twitter feed. If a murder or fatal accident made the news, hacks would rather take the easy path, trawling Facebook for badly spelt tributes to the deceased rather than actually approaching the bereaved relatives. Some Wikipedia contributors delighted in making fanciful additions to pages about celebrities known to be on the verge of death, knowing that a time-strapped obituary writer might snap up the information without bothering to check its veracity.[63]

Of course, newspapers and broadcasters were not the only medium to be affected by Web 2.0. Film also suffered from illegal downloads, as did the music industry. Although Apple's iTunes ensured that musicians would receive some compensation from legal downloads, pioneers such as Napster had successfully persuaded younger fans of their entitlement to hear something for nothing. Moreover, the ability to pick and choose individual tracks transferred an unprecedented amount of power to the consumer, threatening the 40-year-old dominance of the album as the definitive format for recorded popular music.[64]

Meanwhile, in books, Amazon continued to transform the retail scene, while the Espresso Book Machine (which printed and bound books on demand) hinted at similar changes within warehousing and distribution. Technology was changing our expectations and experience, and disrupting traditional business models at every turn. And this state of uncertainty was not restricted to the media. Anything that wasn't in a state of flux was in a state of panic that it soon might be. The devolution of cultural power was not just from blogger to tweeter, or from professional to amateur; it had wider, political implications. Governments realized that they could no longer stop dangerous ideas simply by closing down magazines or radio stations. When, in 2005, Google agreed to self-censor in order to enter the potentially lucrative Chinese market[65] (reasoning that limited access to Google was better than none at all), it provoked such a backlash in its core Western markets that the company's co-founder, Sergey Brin, was compelled to concede that the decision had been 'a net negative'.

But it was not only communist dictatorships that felt threatened. In 2007, the Thai authorities blocked access to YouTube because of a video deemed insulting to the King, and in 2008 the Australian government trialled a system of ISP-level content-filtering – supposedly for the protection of children (though it wasn't clear whether the kids were more at risk from online predators, pornography or the oft-asserted scare story that Facebook use had a negative effect on school grades). In the same year, the Singapore government banned access to the sex video sites YouPorn and RedTube, while acknowledging that this was little more than a symbolic gesture to assert the moral values of the country. Later, in 2009, the Guatemalan authorities arrested a man on a charge of 'inciting financial panic' over a 96-character post on Twitter.

Such interventions were like rearranging deckchairs on the *Titanic*, however, nine times out of 10, a proxy server could bypass such controls. This shift in power was unstoppable. A few weeks after 9/11, the American diplomat Richard Holbrooke pondered; 'How can a man in a cave out-communicate the world's leading communications society?'[66] This remark not only betrayed Holbrooke's lamentable failure to understand the tactics and capabilities of Osama bin Laden but also how the new media were changing the communications landscape in the Noughties.

Since the 1950s, American interests had controlled many of the levers of mass media, such as film, TV and popular music. This meant that the entertainment industry (if often unwittingly) acted as a surreptitious advance guard of US diplomacy; young people around the world adopted (or aspired to adopt) American hairstyles and cars, accents and guitars. It has even been suggested that the upheavals which convulsed the Soviet bloc during the 1980s were prompted in part by *samizdat* copies of *Dallas* and *Dynasty*, offering glimpses of a lifestyle impossible under communism.

In the new world of Web 2.0, however, while most of the key innovations such as Facebook, Twitter and YouTube had begun in the United States, there was no guarantee that their content would originate in America, or be directed at an American audience. In this new world, a Scottish spinster singing a song from a French musical on a British television show could become an international YouTube sensation, attracting more hits for her rendition of 'I Dreamed a Dream' than President Obama received for his election victory speech. As one newspaper columnist noted; 'The reason Susan [Boyle] has been dragged so speedily into the global media slipstream isn't because of telly which, love it as I do, is just so 20th century, but because of the Twitter/YouTube nexus.'[67] When Boyle, in common with other *über*-celebrities, was later referenced in an episode of *The Simpsons*, it was a case of old media playing catch-up with something that was nominally its own creation.

Not all were comfortable with the new reality. When Andrew Schlafly launched Conservapedia as a response to the supposed liberal, secular bias of Wikipedia, one of his gripes was that the latter tolerated British (as opposed to American) spellings; the idea that the majority of internet users were not American seemed beyond his ken.

With the development of Web 2.0, the most powerful nation on Earth had created a lens through which it could watch its cultural dominance slowly disappear.

# Chapter 6

# Are you looking at me?

'You really think you're in control?'
Gnarls Barkley, 'Crazy'

**Spyware** (*noun*) software installed on a computer to collect information without the user's consent (2000)

Despite talk of the internet enabling virtual environments, cutting users off from 'the real world', most technological developments in the Noughties were still related to reality in some way or another. Bloggers, for the most part, blogged about life rather than blogging; even if your Facebook friends weren't always friends in the conventional sense, they were still made of flesh and blood rather than pieces of computer code. The main criticism levelled at Twitter was its mundanity, its minute notation of socks bought and doughnuts consumed.

And if the progress of technology — especially information technology — was one of the big stories of the Noughties, it was inevitable that it would become entangled in the other theme that dominated the decade — the use and abuse of fear. The problem was, it was often difficult to see which was the tail and which was the dog.

It is impossible to consider these interactions without taking into account the events of 9/11 and what happened in their wake. With the US population traumatized and fearful, within days of the attacks anti-terrorist legislation was introduced into Congress then signed into law (as the US Patriot Act[68]) not six weeks later – a breathtakingly fast timeframe that allowed little room for the usual legislative debate.

The Patriot Act offered a stark message about the tactics that Western governments were prepared to use; specifically, the freedoms that the governed would be expected to forfeit in the interests of a supposedly greater freedom. The authorities were given unprecedented powers to monitor and search emails, phone messages and other communications – involving US citizens and non-citizens alike. The government could even acquire such apparently innocuous data as the books that an individual had borrowed from a public library. While many were swept up in the heat of the moment, and supported the new legislation, not everyone was happy with developments. In a remarkable move, New York, the city most profoundly affected by the 9/11 attacks, passed a resolution repudiating the Act.

While governments have always been interested in the minutiae of the lives of those they govern, there was a key difference between, for example, President Nixon's attempts to bug his political enemies in the early 1970s and this new Patriot Act; while Nixon's activities were covert, the Patriot Act was conducted in full view of those who were its potential targets. Concerns about privacy and constitutional rights were brushed aside with the oft-heard mantra; 'If you've nothing to hide, you've nothing to fear'.

But this principle didn't spring fully formed from the rubble of the World Trade Center. Surveillance cameras had in fact become commonplace in many Western cities. Well before the start of the Noughties, CCTV (closed-circuit television) images had become as much part of the cultural narrative as conventional press photographs; think of the grainy footage of heiress Patty Hearst robbing a bank in San Francisco in 1974, the toddler James Bulger walking hand in hand with his adolescent killers in Liverpool in 1993 and the teenage gunmen stalking the corridors of Columbine High School in 1999. In the new decade, these images would be joined by pictures of the rucksack-wielding 7/7 bombers boarding trains to London; a few minutes of taped, tainted fame.

Indeed, it seemed that Britain was the CCTV surveillance capital of the world. By the end of the decade it was estimated that there were more than 4 million CCTV cameras operating in the UK (some 200,000 in London alone), and that an average urban dweller might show up on 300 of them in any given day.[69] No wonder Hard-Fi (a band from the suburban London outpost of Staines) struck a chord with their breakthrough 2005 album *Stars of CCTV*, the title track of which asserts 'and every move that I make gets recorded to tape so somebody up there can keep me safe'.[70]

Of course, security was central to the justification of surveillance, and when the added finesse of facial recognition software made it possible for the police or other authorities to track the movements of any individual of whom they had a decent mugshot, this was – for the most part – meekly accepted.

Part of this acceptance was down to social and economic changes. With the growing privatization of nominally public spaces – shopping and other leisure activities moving away from high streets and main streets to malls and out-of-town centres – if proprietors wanted to pepper their premises with cameras, they were perfectly free to do so; the only feasible form of protest was to stay away. But even this form of avoidance became less possible with the advent in 2005 of Google Earth, which linked together satellite images and high-resolution 'aerial' photographs to create what was effectively a photographic map of the whole planet; like the web, but linking cameras rather than computers. With Google Earth you could survey the top of Mount Everest or fly across the red centre of Australia. On a more modest flight path, you could zoom in on your own house, or that of your neighbour. Google Earth made the whole world more visible, and more accessible; our sense of what was public and what was private began to dissolve.

With the launch of Google Street View (a service that provided high-resolution, street-level photographs of public roads and streets) in the US in May 2007, the lines between what was private and public space became yet more indistinct. Taking the meaning of the word 'public' in public streets literally, Google was perturbed to receive complaints from individuals unintentionally caught on camera. Bowing to public concern, Google later offered to blur all faces and the number plates of cars; their solicitude extended to the face of Colonel Sanders outside branches of KFC.

But this did not stop the criticism coming. When Street View was introduced in the UK in March 2009, concerns were expressed that it would be used by ne'er-do-wells as a tool for identifying properties to burgle rather than, as Google envisioned, by well-to-dos as a tool for identifying properties to purchase. One person's freedom of information was, it seemed, another person's invasion of privacy.[71] Added to this was concern that Google was operating a one-size-fits-all process that didn't take account of local peculiarities; for example, in Japan, the height at which cameras were mounted enabled them actually to see into many homes, and the company was forced to retake thousands of images.

Still, the supporters of increased surveillance could always rely on the widespread fear of crime that became increasingly entrenched as the decade rolled on. Paradoxically, despite the huge rise in the use of surveillance (much of it intended to detect, indeed deter, crime), it seemed we felt more unsafe than ever.

Irrational fears were nothing new, but in the Noughties there seemed to be so many that they merged into a single, non-specific terror that defied categorization. In the UK, for example, paedophiles, terrorists, asylum seekers, drug addicts, welfare mothers and feral youths, bird flu, swine flu, the MMR jab and foot-and-mouth all combined to create a simmering mass that seemed to threaten the very existence of civilized society. It seemed that the void left by the non-appearance of the millennium bug had to be filled by fear – any fear. Incidences of child abuse and violent crime may have remained pretty much static over the decade, but high-profile stories (such as a spate of knife murders in London in 2007 and 2008, involving young people as victims and perpetrators alike) were seized upon in an increasingly competitive media market that claimed only to be reflecting the concerns of its readers and viewers.

When, in 2009, the Republican politician David Norcross declared that he wanted to make Americans 'properly fearful' of the new Obama administration,[72] he was only articulating a policy – scaring people in the public interest – that had been prevalent, albeit unspoken, for most of the decade. An earlier president, Franklin D Roosevelt, had declared that America (and, by extension, the world) had nothing to fear but fear itself. For the political classes in the Noughties, the greatest fear was lack of fear.

Surveillance might have provided some resolution in certain crimes, but horrors were just as likely to go on in private, beyond the reach of the cameras; horrors such as the Fritzl case, in which an Austrian kept his daughter captive for 24 years, raping her and fathering seven children. Should all private homes have been fitted with cameras to prevent such activities? Not that CCTV had prevented the 7/7 bombings. Nor had it prevented the Bulger murder or the Columbine shootings; it just gave us some more images with which to fuel our personal catalogue of nightmares.

Despite some of the obvious flaws in the surveillance mechanism, the public generally acquiesced; after all, 'if you've nothing to hide...' This tacit acceptance of surveillance often reflected deeper fears that many felt unable to voice explicitly, touching as they did on atavistic sensitivities about 'the other' that in the caring, non-judgemental new century we weren't really supposed to feel any more. When, in 2005, young people wearing 'hoodies'[73] were banned from a large shopping centre outside London, it was supposedly to prevent shoplifters and other undesirables hiding their faces from camera. However, it also spoke of a certain nervousness about the prevalence of black-American hip-hop subculture among British teenagers. Similarly, unease about women wearing identity-masking burqas was inextricably bound up with more general worries over immigration, integration, Islamism and terrorism.

Of course, hoodies, Muslims and all those other purported manifestations of unease were part of a convenient 'other'. When 'ordinary' people found themselves on the receiving end of surveillance – for example, in an encounter with a speed camera – the argument about collective security outweighing the right to privacy suddenly appeared to be rather less clear cut. As in the case of shopping centres, cars were environments that were at once public and private; the problem here came at the point where the private (the car) collided with the public (the legal speed limit or, far worse, the unwitting pedestrian).[74]

But this was about more than cars and cameras. White House rhetoric about the War on Terror gave governments the confidence to consider legislation – such as the introduction of identity card systems in the UK, US, Canada, Australia and New Zealand – that would normally have been unthinkable in peacetime. Promoted as a way of securing personal identity – and therefore reducing the risk both of terrorism (though this was always a tenuous extrapolation) and identity theft – few paused to consider that having key personal identifiers stored in one place actually made identity theft easier, and the effects of any such theft far more wide-ranging and severe.

In the UK, the twin threats of crime and terrorism prompted a number of legislative proposals, including the extension of the period of time that a criminal suspect could be held without charge and the sanctioning of police to hold DNA and other evidence from people who had been arrested but never charged, or charged but never convicted – ie the innocent. Following a damning ruling by the European Court of Human Rights in December 2008, which criticized 'the blanket and indiscriminate nature of the power of retention in England and Wales', the British government was forced to back track, though it still foot-dragged over the detail.

Such fundamental changes to the balance of power between state and individual led to some unlikely alliances, not least the partnership between Shami Chakrabati, the left-leaning head of the civil rights pressure group Liberty, and the robustly right-wing shadow Home Secretary David Davis, who resigned his seat in parliament to draw attention to the proposal to extend detention without charge.

Davis was not the only one to raise the alarm. The British newspaper columnist Peter Preston regularly spotlighted the potentially corrosive effect of legislation on privacy and civil liberties, while books such as Kieron O'Hara and Nigel Shadbolt's *The Spy in the Coffee Machine* (2008) highlighted the effect of digital technology. Meanwhile, in Hollywood, the 2006 film *A Scanner Darkly* (based on the 1977 book of the same name by Philip K Dick) described a nightmare vision of a hypersurveillance society 'seven years from now'.

Despite all these expressions of concern, for some people, surveillance was still really rather sexy. The success of the BBC spy drama *Spooks* (aka *MI-5*) prompted a substantial increase in the number of applicants to the security services. While many were doubtless motivated by patriotism, there was something undeniably exciting about tracking, trailing and bugging an unwary individual. The high-tension TV show *24*, the *Bourne* movie franchise and a reinvigorated, muscled-up James Bond had also brought spying back into the mainstream of entertainment. *Spooks*, however, was unusual in that it devoted almost as much time to the backroom geeks with their gadgets, crosswords and repressed homosexuality as it did to the good-looking daredevils; it was as if Q had demanded equal billing with 007.

Apart from generalized anxieties about surveillance, a niggling worry persisted that technological developments could also lead to individuals' personal data ending up in the wrong hands. 'Phishing' (the use of fake emails to elicit financial and other personal details, often under the guise of a security check) and spyware exploded during the Noughties, taking advantage of the fact that the internet transcended borders in ways criminal investigations couldn't manage. With parts of the criminal chain operating in different countries, under different laws, the prosecution of cybercriminals was a bureaucratic nightmare.

If people were wary of governments' access to information, they were positively terrified of the presence on the web of terrorists, child pornographers, drug dealers and organized crime – identified by the cyberpunk author Bruce Sterling as 'the Four Horsemen of the Infocalypse'.[75] After the deadly Mumbai attacks of 2008, the surviving gunman admitted that he'd made use of Google Earth in the planning stages. Once again the point was made; information could be used for good or ill, technology could cut both ways.

It wasn't just criminal elements whose online presence made people queasy. With the stated ambition 'to organize the world's information and make it universally accessible and useful', Google, the folksy, nerdy, devastatingly successful company originally set up by a couple of Stanford University post-grads back in 1998, was keen to get its hands on as much information as possible – particularly information about individuals. In common with all search engines, Google tracked individuals' activities on the web – their digital clickstreams. Tracking users' clickstreams not only enabled Google to deliver more relevant search results but also, crucially, more relevant and targeted ads – revenue from which was the lifeblood of its business.

But Google wanted to get even closer to individuals. Beyond search, Google also offered to store your videos, email and social networking messages, your spreadsheets and WP documents; even your stock portfolio and health records. While these were all useful services in themselves, with so much information on individual citizens concentrated in the hands of one organization, questions inevitably began to be asked about Google, and its intentions; was Google perhaps building a vast database that could be exploited for commercial gain at a later date? What if blackmailers, identity thieves, fraudsters or government snoopers got hold of the data? With so much information, and so much ambition, was Google really going to be able to stay true to its informal company motto – 'Don't be evil'?

Google, however, was not the only one on our tail (or to arouse concern).[76] The new science of behavioural advertising used software which tracked individuals' internet use to allocate the advertisements that might be especially relevant to them. By the end of the Noughties, government and commercial interests could uncover information about our behaviour in a manner that made CCTV look distinctly primitive.

And it was not just our activities on the web that were being tracked; every time we paid with our credit card, drove on a toll road or made a call on our mobile phone, we left behind a digital trail, a trail which – like our clickstream – could be analyzed, interpreted and (potentially) exploited. Once again, the duality of information and technology was exposed. Our mobile might usefully direct us to a cool local bar or source of cheap designer clothing, but it might also broadcast our movements. What if suspicious employers used it to track staff, or suspicious spouses to track partners?

Still, in terms of overt surveillance, it seemed that individuals could always turn the tables. The Canadian academic Steve Mann coined the terms 'sousveillance' and 'inverse surveillance' to describe the increasing tendency of those who were traditionally the objects of surveillance (eg political demonstrators) to use small, inexpensive cameras and other devices to record the actions of the police and other authorities. This technique was particularly associated with anti-capitalist and environmental protestors, and it came to widespread attention in April 2009, in the aftermath of the demonstrations that attended the G20 summit in London.

The official version of events that led to the death of a bystander, Ian Tomlinson, was contradicted by video footage taken by an American fund manager. Further images of police apparently striking non-violent protestors raised serious questions, not simply about police behaviour but also about the integrity of their witness. Tomlinson's death came weeks after the British government had tightened the laws around photographing police officers, giving added piquancy to the pictures of their apparently casual violence. It felt as if government believed it had the right to sift through the digital grit not just of our lives but of the images that represented our lives; was there perhaps a database in London, Washington or Canberra that contained the passwords to all our Flickr accounts?

For a number of reasons, the Noughties saw a renewed interest in the ideas of the author George Orwell, who had died back in 1950. Some of this interest took the form of entertainingly contemporary but ultimately pointless hypotheses. Would Orwell have been in favour of the Iraq War? Would he have been a blogger? What would Orwell have made of the smoking ban? But Orwell the posthumous moral arbiter really came into his own when the subject of surveillance came up. Maybe there should have been something called 'Orwell's Law' which stated that the likelihood of the phrase 'Big Brother society' entering a conversation about speed cameras rose in inverse proportion to the likelihood of the speaker ever having read Orwell's (1949) classic *Nineteen Eighty-Four*, in which he originally explored the concept of citizens under pervasive surveillance and control.

In any case, when you Googled 'Big Brother' in the Noughties you didn't come up with Orwell, you came up with a television programme. In this hugely popular show, thousands of people volunteered to live in front of the cameras, like the good citizens who believed that, because they had nothing to hide, they had nothing to fear. In fact, it could be argued that the Noughties version of the all-seeing eye was even more intrusive that that of the dystopias created in the preceding century. In Yevgeny Zamyatin's *We* (written in 1921), a key precursor to *Nineteen Eighty-Four*, humans live in a glass city, with all their actions visible to 'the Great Benefactor'; only during their prearranged, permitted 'sexual days' do the blinds descend. Contestants in *Big Brother* were not even permitted such a veil of modesty; the camera became a voyeur, deconstructing eye contact and plotting nascent romance. We may have sometimes felt uneasy about the state spying on us in the streets, but it seemed we were quite happy to have strangers surveying what we got up to under the sheets.

For a while, it really did seem that *Big Brother* the TV show was more important than Big Brother the pervasive eye of state power (or its elected representatives). Australian Prime Minister John Howard fulminated about declining moral standards after an apparent sexual assault took place on the show in 2006. The following year, his British counterpart, Gordon Brown, felt obliged to weigh in over the racial abuse of Shilpa Shetty, and then later pay tribute to one of her accused, Jade Goody, as she battled her cancer in front of yet more cameras (Jade and Shilpa having by this point publicly reconciled). Voters of both kinds sniggered and moved on.

And soon they began to move on from *Big Brother* as well. By the time the tenth series of the UK version aired in 2009, audiences had slumped to under 2 million (having been three times higher at the peak of the show's popularity), and many were calling for it to be put out of its misery. But it certainly wasn't because a couple of middle-aged men (of whom many viewers were only vaguely aware) thought it was a bit tacky. Maybe in the light of increasing wariness about the reality of an all-seeing, all-knowing state, that joke just wasn't funny any more. Or maybe it just felt a bit *passé* to present an environment where individuals were unable to watch and record those who watched and recorded them. The Noughties may have brought fresh attention to George Orwell, but it was not his dystopia that warranted revisiting.

In 2008, the BBC showed a remake of *Survivors*, its cult science-fiction TV show from the 1970s about the after-effects of a plague that kills more than 90% of the world's population. The theme was undoubtedly timely in that it chimed with media-driven medical panics that may or may not have been disproportionate, such as those surrounding SARS and swine flu. But there was another thread – that of how people behave in the absence of any functioning government or other infrastructure. There was a key difference in the remake, however; this time round, a secret band of government scientists remained, observing the survivors from an underground location, logging their identities, tracking their movements, reasserting control when events failed to go to plan.

Meanwhile, the US channel AMC commissioned a 'reimagining' of the cult 60s show *The Prisoner*, about an individual (known only as Number Six) who is consigned to a mysterious environment called 'the Village' – a place that is superficially idyllic but ultimately totalitarian. The star of the original show, Patrick McGoohan, died in early 2009, just before the G20 protestors finally learned to throw his smirking pay-off line back in the faces of those who watched from above; 'Be seeing you!'

# Chapter 7
# Shopaholic

'I am a weapon of massive consumption.'

Lily Allen, 'The Fear'

**Metrosexual** (*noun, adjective*) fashion-conscious, well-groomed heterosexual male (2003)

In the immediate aftermath of the 9/11 attacks, many people in the United States and beyond felt deeply frustrated. They may not have been personally affected by the devastation in New York and elsewhere, but they wanted to do something to help, to demonstrate solidarity with the victims and defiance of the attackers. Many gave blood or donated to medical charities, and there was an upsurge in military recruitment. A few weeks after that extraordinary September morning, President Bush offered some guidance to responsible, concerned, patriotic citizens:

> Now, the American people have got to go about their business. We cannot let the terrorists achieve the objective of frightening our nation to the point where we don't conduct business, where people don't shop.[77]

Not all the words Bush spoke during his presidency were well chosen, but this entreaty to hit the malls was very precise. Part of its appeal was a suggestion of normality; a declaration that Americans would not be cowed by terrorist outrages, an echo of the British 'Keep Calm and Carry On' poster. But there was more to it than that; Bush knew that without shopping everything else would fall apart.

Much of America's economic success in the 20th century had been founded on manufacturing; Henry Ford's adoption and refinement of mass-production techniques set a standard for factories around the world. However, from the 1960s onwards, Japanese companies such as Toyota and Sony had begun to offer serious competition. The emphasis in North America and Western Europe shifted towards service industries; the dirty business of actually making stuff increasingly outsourced to places where land and labour were less expensive (and, some argued, employment laws and safety regulations less rigorous).

Globalization – the process by which businesses sought to transcend the notional inconvenience of national borders – had been progressing in fits and starts throughout the previous five decades, but it really started to come into its own (and meet high-profile, coherent opposition) in the 1990s, following the collapse of the Soviet Union. The supporters of globalization argued that it spread the benefits of technology, innovation and free enterprise to all parts of the world, especially to poorer countries. Western enterprises invested in developing nations, bringing employment and training opportunities beyond the means of local businesses; moreover, local partners and franchisees would become wealth-creating entrepreneurs in their own right. It was a virtuous circle; all boats lifting on a rising tide.

The opposing view – as articulated by the likes of Naomi Klein in her 2000 book *No Logo* and Kalle Lasn in the magazine *Adbusters* – was that global corporations were exploiting the poor by setting up badly regulated sweatshops, often bribing local authorities to turn a blind eye to substandard conditions. The extortionate retail price of a pair of Nike sneakers was inevitably contrasted with the pitiful wage offered to the Indonesian teenager who had made them. Moreover, the appearance of global retail concerns such as McDonald's and Starbucks in the developing world was not really creating new employment opportunities; the glossy, branded shops were just forcing out local, independent businesses, the difference being that when a Starbucks replaced an old-style retailer, a slice of valuable turnover made its way back to the West.

At the same time, the proliferation of identikit burger bars and coffee shops was having an insidious cultural impact on developing nations. Popular TV, cinema and music had long been acclaimed and castigated as the hidden persuaders of American hegemony; as the tempo of globalization picked up, they were joined in the campaign by food, drink and clothing, a supposedly benevolent invasion described by its detractors as 'Coca-Colanization'.

However, the invaders knew that they needed to tread carefully; Howard Schultz, the CEO of Starbucks, claimed that 'for us to succeed in China, we have to be Chinese, not American'.[78] And certainly the big American chains made attempts to adapt their generic products to local cultural customs and tastes (eg the McFalafel sandwich in parts of the Middle East and the Teriyaki McBurger in Japan). Still, much of their initial success was down to the cosmopolitan cachet they offered over local, non-branded concerns, the *ersatz* sophistication and exoticism of being non-local. Of course, the same thing had happened when Chinese and other Asian eateries first appeared in the West; but these were mainly small, individual concerns, not global enterprises with big advertising budgets and large capital resources.

A Chinese Starbucks may not have been a carbon copy of an American one, but it wasn't exactly a traditional Chinese tea shop either. Increasingly, these branded environments became a place apart; you were neither in Shanghai, Sydney nor Seattle but in 'Starbucksland', a deracinated nation with its own transcendent identity, a strange synthesis of all the coffee shops you'd ever been in around the world, but not quite like any of them. Again, this process has parallels with Asian restaurants in Europe and elsewhere, where the food bears little relation to any authentic Chinese, Indian or other cuisine. The process of distancing American brands from American-ness became increasingly important as the Noughties progressed; as US foreign policy became ever more unpopular, companies such as KFC sought to downplay their origins in international markets.

But it wasn't only in the developing world that these big brands dominated the cultural scene. The process was even more advanced in the West, where local and independent retailers were increasingly being squeezed out by chains and big retailers. Shops that had served their communities for generations (often under the ownership of the same family) found themselves unable to compete with the deep pockets and economies of scale commanded by the big players; the newcomers often had sufficient capital to absorb any initial losses, drawing custom from the incumbent businesses on the basis of low prices and special offers (which were quickly withdrawn once the competition had been seen off).

Still, there were exceptions. In 2008, Starbucks was forced to close some 70% of its stores in Australia; the Aussies' strong culture of independent cafés, as well as popular local brands such as Hudsons in Melbourne, making it difficult for Starbucks to capture the following it required.

Nonetheless, as a rule, wherever you pitched up in the Western world, you were likely to find the same stock sold under the same sign, with staff who looked pretty much identical whichever branch you visited (and who usually had the same thoroughly drilled sales patter). These 'cloned' high streets gave no clue as to the history or geography of the area; you could have been in New Jersey or New Mexico, in Edinburgh or Exeter.[79]

That was assuming, of course, that the traditional high street or main street was still the sort of place people wanted to shop. The American model of 'big box' out-of-town superstores (as epitomized by the giant Wal-Mart) spread to Europe and beyond, further threatening many towns' increasingly fragile sense of identity and community. Often only accessible by car, if you were without personal transport, you were out of the loop.

While some vociferously protested against the march of the supermarkets, and books such as Bill Quinn's *How Wal-Mart is Destroying America (and the world)* (2000) and Andrew Simms' *Tescopoly* (2007) detailed their ills, their progress seemed all but unstoppable. A vociferous minority of consumers aspired to sedate, well-mannered rebellion and spent their cash at the increasing number of farmers' markets, or on organic box schemes. But this was mere pocket money compared to the huge sums pulled in by the supermarkets.

And there were other concerns. The world's three biggest supermarket chains – Wal-Mart (from the US), Carrefour (France) and Tesco (UK) – were not just swallowing up the direct competition (Wal-Mart taking over the British Asda in 1999 for example) and forcing small, independent stores to close down, they were also, in a sense, closing down our experience. Selling everything from clothes to furniture, books to toys and music to DVDs, why should we bother going anywhere else? Sure, they might have only been the bestselling music CDs or the latest mass-market paperbacks, but at these prices, who cared?

Meanwhile, back on the high street, the units previously oc- cupied by independent butchers, bakers and booksellers were taken over by charity and remainder shops – haunts of an underclass that hadn't been invited to the party. Of course, if you did ever feel the urge to shop on your local high street or main street (or even around the corner), retailers like Tesco had that covered too with their special format 'Metro' and 'Express' stores. And you could always go online.

Inevitably, the effects of supermarket dominance extended far beyond shoppers – to suppliers. To meet supermarket demands, farmers not only had to grow fruit and vegetables on a suitable scale but anything they did grow had to fit strict specifications, including the ability to be harvested, processed and trans- ported easily. All these parameters encouraged conformity and homogeneity; in the UK, the supermarkets effectively reduced over 1,200 varieties of native apples down to two – Bramley and Cox. Were supermarkets, the modern retail equivalent of the Turkish bazaar, actually reducing consumer choice?

Suppliers were also squeezed on margin. In the absence of serious competition, retailers found it easy to dictate prices, constantly pushing suppliers in a bid to keep shopfloor prices low. For most of the decade, the five biggest British supermarket chains could boast higher combined profits than all of the UK's 230,000 farms put together.[80] The emphasis on pushing up margin also forced down wages, to the extent that many farmers in North America and Western Europe could only afford to pick their crops with the aid of (often illegal) immigrant labour, leading to additional social tensions. The same thing happened with overseas suppliers, although here the stakes were often higher; a single buyer's decision to accept or reject a Kenyan farmer's harvest of green beans could fundamentally affect the lives of an entire community. Not that green beans were an indigenous Kenyan crop, or a traditional part of the local diet; they were introduced and grown especially for Western markets.

Superficially, the supermarkets had a reasonable response to these criticisms – nobody was forced to shop at a big, out-of-town superstore as opposed to a local, independent greengrocer, fishmonger or record store. But this assumes that shoppers were making rational, informed decisions, and the evidence suggests that this wasn't always the case.

Western consumers had seemingly become addicted to consumption; enjoying the endorphin-driven rush of acquisition, they sought to reclaim the feeling time and again (retailers egging them on with exhortations to 'Buy now while stocks last!'). It also seemed that consumers had lost any sense of how products actually came to line the supermarket shelves and end up in their shopping baskets. Like decadent pharaohs, they demanded strawberries in the depths of winter, as if they were an inalienable right. The fact that said strawberries tasted of very little (many having been bulked out with water to meet weight criteria) was neither here nor there; if consumers wanted them, they got them. The question of who might have made that bargain T-shirt, or how that bargain chicken might have been forced to live its brief life, was irrelevant.

Or was it? Throughout the decade, consumers claimed to care deeply about the social, economic and environmental impact of their shopping. Retailers were able to command a healthy premium for anything labelled green, ethical, organic, free range or Fairtrade (or any combination thereof). As the language of food miles and carbon footprints gained traction, 'local' became the new buzzword (although the definition of local – as with some of the other labels – was elastic; some supermarket produce making extensive round trips due to centralized distribution). Seasonality also got a push with, for example, the launch in Britain of the 'Eat Seasonably' campaign in May 2009 (supported, of course, with its own labelling).

Meanwhile, big brands such as Nike attempted to repair their damaged reputations with conspicuous acts of corporate social responsibility, while McDonald's boasted of Rainbow Alliance-certified coffee. Even the voracious Wal-Mart embraced a sustainability agenda, promising to cut packaging and reduce waste, energy use and greenhouse gas emissions. Tesco introduced 'green points' to their highly successful loyalty card scheme. Others, such as the French cosmetics giant L'Oréal, looked for reflected glory, buying up the British ethical cosmetics chain the Body Shop in 2006. In a less obvious move, Clorox, a company best known for its bleach products, purchased Burt's Bees, the 'Earth-friendly, natural personal care company', at the end of 2007.

But you had to be a little careful. When Dick Olver, Chairman of weapons manufacturer BAE Systems, announced to shareholders that the group was dedicated to becoming a leader in ethics, his words were met with hisses and boos, one investor accusing him of Orwellian spin; 'A world leader in weapons, yes, but not in ethics.' Similar eyebrows were raised at the start of the decade when transnational oil giant British Petroleum shortened its name to 'BP' and adopted a new slogan – 'Beyond Petroleum'. It also adopted a new corporate insignia; out went the serious-looking shield and in came a cheerful green, white and yellow 'sunburst'.

Beyond all this corporate 'greenwash', when it came to actually choosing products to buy, cost and convenience usually trumped everything, at least when it came to food. The 2008 credit crunch didn't help matters, with many customers switching to value lines or discount stores. Even if cost was not a shopper's primary concern, the lack of a single, coherent and comprehensive labelling system (in the UK at least) made it difficult for consumers to make the 'right' choice – to decide between organic and local, ethical and green.

Aspiration and action also diverged when it came to shopping for clothes. TV viewers (especially women) drooled over the acquisitive lifestyles of the characters in *Sex and the City*, with its fetishization of designer desirables such as Manolo Blahnik footwear. And yet the real retail boom was not in the luxury end of the market but in high-fashion, low-price brands such as Zara from Spain and Primark (nicknamed 'Primarni') from Ireland. With shops such as Zara, designs were on the catwalk one day and in a physical store the next. Keen to encourage repeat footfall, the company worked on the basis of producing limited batches, so that popular items automatically became scarce and customers never knew exactly what would be available. A boon for the style-conscious, this 'fast fashion' model was not so great for the environmentally-conscious; designed with obsolescence in mind, large amounts of clothing ended up in landfill.

In the Noughties, high end did not necessarily mean high status. Movie stars were still to be seen sporting Gucci or D&G, but their fans were often quite brazen about buying their designer gear at discount stores such as TJ Maxx (known in Europe, for some reason, as TK Maxx), or just acquiring bootleg versions. In fact, there was a certain cachet to be had from wielding a fake Louis Vuitton bag or rip-off Donna Karan jacket, acquired on a Far Eastern holiday. This was something the psychotic yuppie Patrick Bateman (from Bret Easton Ellis' 1991 novel *American Psycho*) would never have understood. While Bateman meticulously itemized the brands of his clothes, gadgets and skincare products, by the time the movie version of the book arrived (in 2000), all the must-haves had become generic.

When it came to fashion in the Noughties, the only rule was no rules. Whereas 1970s fashion could roughly be bounded by punk and platforms, and 60s fashion by hippy and mod, in the Noughties pretty much anything went – vintage with Versace, Armani with Aldi. A hit film from 2006 might have assured us that the devil wears Prada, but in the real world, it seemed, his disciples were just as happy to be wearing Primark. So happy, in fact, that Primark and other value stores rode out the 2008 credit crunch pretty well.

At least when it came to choosing between clothes brands, there were fewer ethical issues at stake; both luxury and budget lines were usually created by low-paid workers with few employment rights, often, in fact, in the very same factories. And these factories were not necessarily to be found outside Europe or the West. In 2007, the Italian TV documentary *Schiavi del Lusso* (*Slaves of Luxury*) exposed the dire conditions endured by low-wage workers (mostly from China) in the Tuscan town of Prato; suddenly, a 'Made in Italy' label didn't quite have the same appeal.

In truth, despite the millions spent on advertising products (not just via traditional media such as TV and radio but increasingly via text messages to mobiles, rolling banner and video ads on websites, and contextual ads on search engine pages), the merchandise itself was really only of secondary importance. What was being sold was shopping itself – the excitement, the fantasy, the pursuit, the feeling of guilty self-indulgence. Shoppers may have joked about the benefits of 'retail therapy' but research increasingly found that impulsive or irrational purchases masked deeper emotional turmoil; depressed people were twice as likely to buy things they really didn't need or even want, and many people regretted their purchases the next day.[81] The parallels with casual sex were all too obvious. It was the transaction that brought happiness; the item itself could just hang reproachfully in the wardrobe.

Consumers were paying for something that had only a tentative relationship with reality – design, branding, service, status, the experience. When you thought you were buying a pair of trainers from Nike, only a small proportion of the money you handed over actually went on the shoes themselves; you were really buying 'the swoosh' – 'Just do it', Michael Jordan, Tiger Woods. The mission of Starbucks was not to sell you a caffeinated beverage but, according to *The Green Apron Book* (handed out to all staff members), 'to provide an uplifting experience that enriches people's daily lives'. As Howard Schultz put it; 'What people fail to understand is that we do not just sell a cup of coffee...every single day, Starbucks brings people together.'[82] Customers were paying not so much for the coffee but for the feeling that the coffee (and the armchairs, the chalkboards and the spurious atmosphere of bohemianism) gave them.

The irony in Schultz's credo was that, despite the female bonding celebrated by *Sex and the City*, most shopping (whether for clothes, medicines or food) had ceased to be a 'together' experience. Where shoppers had once built personal relationships with their tailor, their pharmacist, their grocer, now the most they could expect from the underpaid checkout assistant was a standard request to 'come again'; assistants were not encouraged to indulge in idle banter. Paradoxically, there was actually more community to be had in the virtual world of online shopping; successful digital enterprises such as Amazon (which sold more than just books) and eBay (which sold more or less everything) positively encouraged users to discuss the merits or otherwise of the products on offer, while price comparison websites offered the financial lowdown. This exchange of views was clearly as much an attempt to build a sense of togetherness and community as it was an attempt to empower individual opinion. After all, as author Michael Bywater sighed; 'The reviews on Amazon are as powerful an argument against democracy as you could ever find.'[83]

But there was a problem. Just as consumers seemed unable – or unwilling – to think about the origins of the things they bought (if indeed it was 'things' they were actually buying), they also seemed to be in denial about how they were going to pay for them. It was strangely appropriate that people were paying for something that didn't really exist with money that didn't really exist either. Years of easy credit (available to governments and businesses as well as individuals) had severed any tangible connection between spending and earning. If shoppers were having their credit cards turned down, it wasn't just retailers that suffered; producers – most visibly General Motors – also hit the wall.

President Bush's entreaty to the people of America to keep shopping so as to keep the economy moving only made sense in the long term if the money being spent was real. But the retail boom was based on a proportion of cheap credit that was unsustainable, and the whole thing began to unravel in dramatic fashion during Bush's second term (see Chapter 10).

The President's supporters might have argued that he was simply fulfilling his role as a cheerleader for American consumer capitalism, lifting the spirits of his people in a time of fear and despondency. Others, such as the academic Andrew Bacevich, were less forgiving, seeing Bush's entreaties as a conscious attempt to distract the voters from his increasingly counterproductive adventures in the Middle East, the sort of deft misdirection that conjurers have employed for centuries:

> Bush seems to have calculated – cynically but correctly – that prolonging the credit-fuelled consumer binge could help keep complaints about his performance as commander-in-chief from becoming more than a nuisance. Members of Congress calculated – again correctly – that their constituents were looking to Capitol Hill for *largesse*, not lessons in austerity. In this sense, recklessness on main street, on Wall Street and at both ends of Pennsylvania Avenue proved mutually reinforcing.[84]

But hey, who listens to academics anyway? In April 2009, as unemployment and repossessions rocketed, companies folded and banks begged for handouts, the British fashion chain Topshop opened a new branch in New York. Shoppers queued around the block, attracted not just by the appearance of the model Kate Moss (who also designed for the store), or even necessarily by the reasonably priced clothes, but by the opportunity of all that retail therapy. After all, hadn't they earned it?

# Chapter 8

# And the band played on

'Appliances have gone berserk.'
Radiohead, 'Last Flowers'

**Bastard pop** (*noun*) a composition created by blending two or more musical pieces into a single work, usually without the permission of the copyright holder (2001)

From ragtime to ragga, for much of the 20th century our lives played out against a specific, almost clichéd, soundtrack. Think 60s, think Motown, the Beatles and the Elvis comeback. Think 70s, think Led Zeppelin, Abba, glam, punk and disco. Part of this, of course, was down to the influence of film-makers, who knew that a quick blast of Jimi Hendrix would transport us back to a lazy, hazy Woodstockian 60s more surely than any specific textual reference. But there was more to it than this; for much of the 20th century, music (most particularly pop music) was a shared experience, an expression of both unity and dissent.

So where does this leave the Noughties? If the decade had a soundtrack at all, it was a strangely subdued one. There were a number of reasons for this, but perhaps the most significant was that — however resonant and revolutionary the music (and people were still making good music in the Noughties) — it wasn't as transformative as the technological innovations that were convulsing the industry. This truly was a time when the medium made more noise than the message.

Since the 1960s, the music industry had pursued a defined purpose — to sell pre-packaged units of recorded sound. It was a business (albeit a creative one), and some took this to its logical extremes; Berry Gordy's Motown spitting out records from its legendary Studio A in Detroit like cars from a production line. The Four Tops, Stevie Wonder, Marvin Gaye and Tammi Terrell were flesh-and-blood Cadillacs. Later, in the 1980s, the British producers Stock, Aitken, Waterman took the same approach, launching artists such as Kylie Minogue, to less critical acclaim but similar financial success.

Occasionally, the specific details of the industry changed — the displacement of shellac 78 rpm discs by vinyl in the 1950s, the shift in importance from singles to albums in the late 60s and early 70s, and the arrival of compact discs in the 1980s — but the business model remained the same. Every other aspect of the industry — radio play, press coverage, promotional videos, even live performance — was evaluated according to how many units were shifted, most of them in dedicated record shops. In the Noughties, this all fell to pieces.

The roots of this disintegration lie as far back as the late 1980s when German and American scientists worked on developing what would become known as the 'MP3 file', a means of compacting digital sound to a convenient size without losing too much of the significant data. This was even before the development of the web, and it was not until the late 1990s — when internet usage became more widespread and connections faster and more efficient – that the technology was able to get up and bite the complacent backside of the music business. In 1998, a student named Shawn Fanning created Napster, a network that allowed anyone to share any MP3 with anyone else, provided they had some kind of access to the internet. Access to the network was free, and because no payment was made to the copyright holders, the publishers, musicians or record companies, it was illegal. Under intense pressure from the industry, Napster was eventually forced to close in 2001, but the damage had already been done. Napster had not just changed the rules of the game, it had thrown away the board. Napster's impact had been as much social and behavioural as technological; despite the lawsuits, listeners had become used to getting music for free, and now they felt entitled to it.[85]

While Napster returned in 2003, in strictly legitimate form, others (such as Pirate Bay,[86] the Swedish bootlegging site) would soon take over its outlaw mantle.

In the meantime, record companies attempted to launch their own legal download services, but a combination of mutual hostility and shortsighted greed meant that none of them offered the range of products or the flexibility of use that Napster had provided. It was not until Apple launched iTunes at the beginning of 2001 (Amazon MP3 coming later) that consumers had the opportunity to access a legal download service that had anything like the range provided by a conventional record shop. But the iTunes' catalogue did have a few conspicuous gaps, notably the Beatles and AC/DC, who deliberately held back from involvement. This was not so much old-school denial of new opportunities as a desire to protect lucrative CD sales. According to the International Federation of the Phonographic Industry, despite not being available to download (legally), AC/DC's *Black Ice* album was the second biggest selling of 2008, behind Coldplay's *Viva la Vida*.

Still, in many ways, iTunes did offer a distinct advantage over the traditional record shop. When you handed over your cash at Sam Goody or Our Price (neither of which survived the decade) you were getting a selection of music that was predetermined by someone else. CD technology allowed you to juggle the order, maybe even skip some tracks, but if you purchased an album you were still paying for 10, 12 or 20 tracks, not all of which you might necessarily want (and many of which were probably not very good). Even singles, a format that had chugged on despite its increasing financial irrelevance to the industry, were often bulked out by filler.

With iTunes, the basic unit of currency was not the album or the single but the track. Customers were able to buy entire albums, or else cherry pick the best bits, concocting their own stripped-down, all-killer, no-filler greatest hits compilations of an artist or genre. Music obsessives of the type depicted in Nick Hornby's 1995 novel *High Fidelity* were now able to take their chosen art form – the home-made compilation tape – into uncharted territory. Apple's launch of the iPod in October 2001[87] made it easy to create a personalized soundtrack to fit every day, every situation and every mood. Content and running order could be determined by era, genre, lyrical theme or random shuffle. The user, not the record executive, was in charge.

Many developments during the Noughties – from the precipitous decline in the status of the music press to the mid-Noughties boom in MySpace (the preferred medium for musicians acting as their own PR department) and the renewed importance of live performance – can be attributed to this shift in the balance of power. Where once a tour was a vehicle for raising the profile of a new album, by the end of the Noughties, established artists such as Paul McCartney and Madonna had turned this model on its head.

Indeed, contrary to reports of its anticipated death, live performance remained very much alive in the Noughties. Rather than diminishing the appeal of live, artist exposure via YouTube[88] and other sites seemed to stimulate demand; the web was not a rival to live performance but an aid to it – a vital and vibrant publicity tool. Similarly, when (in 2007) a new album from Prince was bundled with copies of a British Sunday newspaper, the singer didn't make any money on the deal, but his follow-up London concerts sold out.

The live festival scene also flourished, from old favourites such as Lollapalooza to upstarts including All Tomorrow's Parties and Latitude. Glastonbury, the largest greenfield music and performing arts festival in the world, also thrived – though perhaps at the cost of its hippy credentials. This was no longer a festival you could attend by hopping over (or diving under) a fence. From about 2002 onwards, security and ticketing at Glastonbury were significantly tightened. Still, once in, you could just chill in the circus field, have a dance at the silent disco or a laugh in the comedy tent. And there was always the music.

Increasingly outflanked by emerging artists from the web, and losing money to free downloads, the big music labels were forced to play safe, cutting rosters and only signing artists who would make them money. However, as the decade marched on, some started to recognize and reach out for new opportunities. In May 2007, CBS bought the UK-based internet radio and community website Last.fm, while labels also signed up to Spotify, the high quality (and fast) music-streaming service. Revenue was secured through a variety of means – subscription, advertising, even donations. This was all well and good (and the arrival late in the decade of big players such as Microsoft on the digital scene reflected the increasing potential of such business models), but it was still a far cry from the good old days.

With the traditional music business on the back foot, artists could now exert more control – provided they took the initiative. Whereas in the past, a fanbase was built up through radio play and advertising (paid for by the label), sites such as MySpace now allowed artists to be in control of their own marketing – at minimal cost. The first video by the British indie/grime band Hadouken!, for example, was far from big budget but still achieved impressive playtime on MTV. Bands could now exist on relatively tiny record (and download) sales, bolstered by heavy gigging and merchandising, all of it coordinated via MySpace, Facebook and Twitter, and disseminated via YouTube and iTunes.

A record deal was an optional extra. In 2009, indie-rockers the Boxer Rebellion became the first unsigned band to have an album in the Billboard Top 100 after their track 'Evacuate' featured as a free single of the week on iTunes. Kate Walsh, on the other hand, was happy to be picked up by Mercury Records after becoming the first unsigned artist to top the UK iTunes album chart. But the DIY ethic could sometimes turn out to be more style than substance; the webcast concerts that propelled Scottish singer Sandi Thom to the top of the British and Australian charts in 2006 were masterminded by a good old-fashioned PR company.

The technology that underpinned these new methods of promotion and distribution also had a profound effect on the creation and production of the music itself. Sampling – the process of incorporating elements of one recording into another – had been around at least since 1928, when American novelty duo the Happiness Boys released 'Twisting the Dials', which incorporated snippets of contemporary hits. In the late 1960s, the art of live mixing was developed simultaneously in the sound systems of Jamaica and the gay discos of New York, a synthesis that evolved into what we know as hip hop. This was closely followed by sonic collagists such as Steinski, M/A/R/R/S, the KLF and the Australian group the Avalanches; according to industry legend, it took longer to get copyright clearance for the 3,500 samples on the latter's 2000 album *Since I Left You* than it did to make the recording itself.

The arrival of Napster, and the ready availability of pretty much any music ever recorded, made it possible to assemble works in which everything was a 'found sound', and nothing whatsoever was original. These postmodern mash-ups (usually blending the vocal line of one song with the rhythm track of another) reached a mass audience when Kylie Minogue blended her own hit 'Can't Get You Out of My Head' with New Order's 1980s floor-filler 'Blue Monday' at the Brit Awards in 2002. But, for the most part, mash-ups such as Freelance Hellraiser's 'A Stroke of Genius' (Christina Aguilera eyeballing the Strokes, 2001), Girls on Top's 'I Wanna Dance with Numbers' (Whitney Houston stuck in a lift with Kraftwerk, also 2001) and Danger Mouse's *The Grey Album* (Jay-Z gets jiggy with the Beatles, 2004) were strictly illegal productions, with limited commercial potential, beyond promoting the abilities of their creators.[89]

Some established artists welcomed the lateral thinking behind mash-up culture. Beck, who had been a 'victim' of the process

(Illegal Art's *Deconstructing Beck* in 1998), felt that it was time to redefine the strict identity of 'the album', especially since bootleggers and downloaders were already doing this unofficially. Musicians had taken nearly two decades to take full advantage of the potential of the vinyl long-play record, and Beck identified a similar lack of courage and imagination when it came to pushing back the boundaries of digital recording. As he put it in 2006:

> There are so many dimensions to what a record can be these days. Artists can and should approach making an album as an opportunity to do a series of releases – one that's visual, one that has alternate versions and one that's something the listener can participate in or arrange and change. It's time for the album to embrace the technology.[90]

But Beck's was something of a lone voice. Even as technology made the notion of a long-play record with a fixed sequence of tracks seem *passé*, there was a resurgence in what could only be called concept albums – the Flaming Lips' *Yoshimi Battles the Pink Robots* (2002), Green Day's *American Idiot* (2004) and *The Liberty of Norton Folgate* by Madness (2009) each offered a coherent(ish) narrative, a whole that was more than the sum of its parts.

Another unlikely (and counterintuitive) Noughties resurgence was vinyl records. Supposedly dealt a mortal blow first by the CD and then by MP3, vinyl (particularly in limited-edition format) found a new market. Unlike anonymous digital, analogue vinyl could be touched, loved and admired; it appealed to the avid bedroom collector in us all. Perhaps even more surprisingly, limited-run cassette tapes also staged a revival late in the decade.

So much for revivals, what of innovations? While earlier musical expressions were often tied to specific socio-economic circumstances (soul music as a manifestation of increased confidence among black Americans, in parallel with the Civil Rights movement; New Romanticism as a reaction against the dreariness of Thatcherite policies in the early 80s), music trends in the Noughties just seemed to happen, trundle along for a bit and then disappear.

If the preceding decade had been defined by dance music (grunge and Britpop notwithstanding), the early Noughties saw a resurgence of credible guitar rock, spearheaded by groups such as the Strokes and the White Stripes, both of whom achieved success in the UK as well as their native US. Suddenly, the airwaves were swamped with guitars. Bands as diverse as the Libertines, Franz Ferdinand, Arctic Monkeys and Kings of Leon were lumped together as 'indie music', essentially rendering the term and the genre meaningless. As a succession of art-school graduates meshed jangly guitars with affectations of melancholia, the club promoter Ian Watson dubbed the phenomenon 'hair metal', a far from complimentary analogy with the over-coiffed commercial rockers of the 1980s.[91]

Meanwhile (if this wasn't enough), the dedicated fan could always kick up a storm in the comfort of his own living room with the popular music video game *Guitar Hero*; the Noughties equivalent of playing a tennis racquet in front of the mirror.

Dance music as a phenomenon wasn't dead of course, and new genres abounded. One of the most exciting was 'grime', a fast, brutal fusion of garage and dancehall that developed in some of the rougher parts of east London, and came to mainstream attention in 2003, thanks to performers such as Dizzee Rascal, Lady Sovereign and Lethal Bizzle. As was often the case with manifestations of 'urban' music, grime attracted criticism for its violent lyrics and its association with gang lifestyles.

Far more palatable to the mass media was the sudden rise, towards the end of the Noughties, of a succession of British female singers, some of whom had the audacity to repeat their success in the United States. Amy Winehouse accrued more column inches for her chaotic Camden lifestyle than for her undoubted musical talent, but performers such as Duffy, Adele and Jamelia had a happier time, and Leona Lewis even had the temerity to top the US single and album charts as well as achieve success in Australia, Japan and many other countries. In a deliciously postmodern moment, Lewis achieved spectacular worldwide exposure when she (the epitome of manufactured Noughties pop) joined Jimmy Page of Led Zeppelin (the epitome of 70s hard-rock authenticity) to perform 'Whole Lotta Love' in front of an estimated global audience of 150 million, for the closing ceremony of the 2008 Beijing Olympics. Pop had eaten itself yet again.

Lewis, who had won series three of *The X Factor*, was one of the few contestants (American Kelly Clarkson being another) to buck the reality show trend of a hugely successful initial single release followed by a rapid return to obscurity. However, the sheer number of these talent shows made it possible to identify a particular style that seemed most likely to impress judges and voters alike – breathy, emotional delivery and plenty of melismatic warbling. The addition of *America's/Britain's Got Talent* to the crowded schedules at least offered some respite from the Mariah Carey wannabes, with tenors Paul Potts and Neal E Boyd claiming titles. Their opera-with-the-boring-bits-taken-out style became known as 'classical crossover', another successful genre during the decade, with singers Charlotte Church and Katherine Jenkins, and the quartets G4 and Il Divo, racking up impressive sales, much to the chagrin of 'real' classical lovers.

The sales achieved by acts such as Il Divo were a belated reminder to the industry that it wasn't only teenagers who bought music; moreover, older music fans were less likely to indulge their desires via the medium of free, illegal downloads. The increasing significance of older fans goes some way towards explaining the number of reunions that occurred in the Noughties. Take That, the Spice Girls, the Police, ABC, the Specials, Duran Duran and Spandau Ballet all overcame age, inertia and mutual loathing to get back together on stage or in the studio. In 2004/2005, fans were subjected to the aesthetic overload of Chicago and Earth, Wind & Fire on the same bill. Meanwhile, acts that had never really gone away – such as the Rolling Stones and U2 – continued to give the punters what they wanted, clocking up huge revenues for themselves in the process. But sometimes it was all too much, Michael Jackson's strenuous preparations for his 50 sold-out shows at London's O2 Arena reputedly contributing to his death.

Things were a little more dignified in the world of classical music. In December 2008, after a long and distinguished career, the concert pianist Alfred Brendel took his final bow, hoping no doubt to spend more time pursuing his five identified essentials for a good life – architecture with round arches, the grotesque, love, a comfortable bed and silence. Meanwhile, 'the Three Tenors' – Plácido Domingo, Luciano Pavarotti and José Carreras – who had shot to popular fame following their appearance on the eve of the 1990 World Cup final in Rome, also exited stage left; Pavarotti died in 2007.

In the Noughties, it seemed as if the idea of a musical genre being associated with a specific youth subculture (as had been the case with punk rock for example) was old hat. The only real exception was the tribe/style known as 'emo', characterized by dark clothing, exaggerated eye make-up, angular fringes and expressions of adolescent angst. Emo (short for emotional) had emerged as long ago as the mid-1980s — as an offshoot from the US hardcore rock scene — but it was not until the early Noughties that bands such as Jimmy Eat World turned it into a global phenomenon. Within a few years, however, emo had become as much a pejorative term as a tag to be welcomed, and the likes of Fall Out Boy and My Chemical Romance repudiated any association with the term. Emo became a catch-all descriptor for any behaviour characteristic of a sensitive teenager, with specific reference to self-absorption and alienation; as the critic Paul Morley noted, the success of emo as a socio-musical signifier lies in the fact that, ultimately, 'it doesn't mean anything'.[92]

And as emo became an embarrassment, for the first time in about 50 years it was all but impossible to guess what music teenagers enjoyed just by looking at their clothes. As with the Walkman and Discman before it, the iPod turned music into a solitary, essentially private passion; you might be dressed in full emo regalia but nobody else need know you were listening to Il Divo. The iPod evangelist Dylan Jones described it thus:

> Unlike every other aspect of the computer world, the iPod had little to do with togetherness, had little to do with community spirit. The iPod was all about individuality and personal space, and its marketing would soon reflect that.[93]

So, with music and youth culture fragmented into any number of personal spaces, how can the musical landscape of the decade be summed up? A chart seems appropriate, although the social significance of such a concept waned during the Noughties, and the long-running British TV show *Top of the Pops* bit the dust. But this isn't a chart based on sales figures, nor is it some attempt to define the 'best' records of the decade. It is just a few records that go some way towards encapsulating the period. So, in the best chart countdown tradition, here's my Top Five.

### Number 5: Danger Mouse, *The Grey Album* (2004)

*The Grey Album* – the work that established the notoriety of Brian 'Danger Mouse' Burton – represents a clash of musical generations and business mindsets. Like most mash-ups, it was never intended to be a commercial hit; Burton's original intention was to release 3,000 copies to showcase his production talents. As the title hints, his raw materials were an *a cappella* mix of Jay-Z's *The Black Album* (released the previous year) and the Beatles' eponymous double LP from 1968, better known as *The White Album*.

The Jay-Z album was specifically created to encourage experiments such as Burton's, on the basis that such remixes and mash-ups could only serve to raise the profile of the original work, just as the exhaustive plundering of James Brown's back catalogue by hip-hop artists in the 1980s had encouraged renewed interest in the funk pioneer. The Beatles (or, more precisely, their record company EMI, who held the copyright for *The White Album*) were not amused however, and threatened legal action. Rather than cravenly siding with the music industry big hitters, the mainstream media admired both Burton's skills and his *chutzpah*; *Entertainment Weekly* named *The Grey Album* its album of the year.

Burton's impudent release had its desired effect, making its creator one of the most in-demand producers of the Noughties; he went on to work with Damon Albarn and Beck, both of whom shared his fascination with disrupting the conventional dynamics of the music business. In 2006, Gnarls Barkley, the duo Burton formed with singer Cee-Lo Green, released the single 'Crazy'. Apart from its contemporary mood of paranoia and distraction, it became the first single to top the British single charts without having been released in physical form.

In 2009, Burton found himself embroiled in conflict with EMI once again, when the release of his *Dark Night of the Soul* album (a collaboration with Sparklehorse, film-maker David Lynch and a host of other left-field legends) was held up by undisclosed legal disagreements. In its place, Burton announced that he was going to release a blank, recordable compact disc, packaged with Lynch's artwork. Since by this point the album could be downloaded from any number of websites, the implication (for both listeners and the music business) was fairly plain.

## Number 4: Alexandra Burke (and others), 'Hallelujah' (1984)

As throughout the Noughties pop music became increasingly postmodern and self-referential, it was oddly refreshing to encounter that terribly old-fashioned phenomenon, a song that everyone wanted to sing. They used to be called 'standards' of course; Irving Berlin, Cole Porter or Richard Rodgers would come up with a catchy tune, it would be slotted into a Broadway show and, within weeks, everyone from Frank Sinatra down would have recorded a version.

But then came a time when singers could only maintain credibility if they wrote their own material. The occasional cover version was permissible, but it had to be a song that nobody else had attempted for a while; the idea of half a dozen singers all releasing versions of the same song was unthinkable, even shameful.

And then 'Hallelujah' happened.

Actually, 'Hallelujah' first happened as long ago as 1984, when its composer, the Canadian singer-songwriter Leonard Cohen, included it on his album *Various Positions*. John Cale recorded a radically different version of the song in 1991, based on revisions that Cohen had made when playing the song live in the intervening years. Cale's is the version heard on the soundtrack to the movie *Shrek* (2001). In 1994, the song appeared on Jeff Buckley's album *Grace*; kd lang and Rufus Wainwright also had a go.

It was not until 2006, however, that 'Hallelujah' fever really took hold. The process began in Norway, where the singer Kurt Nilsen (a former winner of Norway's *Pop Idol*, and subsequently of *World Idol*) formed a supergroup under the unwieldy title the New Guitar Buddies; their version of 'Hallelujah' subsequently topped the Norwegian charts. The 'Idol' connection was reinforced with performances by Amanda Jenssen on the Swedish version of the show in 2007 and Jason Castro on *American Idol* in 2008; but it was Alexandra Burke who had the most success, winning the 2008 series of Britain's *The X Factor* and grabbing the still-coveted Christmas number one spot. An online campaign by musical purists, angered by the *faux*-gospel arrangement of Burke's version, also dragged the Buckley and Cohen versions into the Top 40. In the meantime, everyone from AOR veteran Jon

Bon Jovi to crossover mezzo Katherine Jenkins took a crack at 'Hallelujah', with varying results.

So, what was it about this particular song that appealed to fans of schlocky talent shows, indie-rock martyrs and green ogres alike? Well, it's got a pretty tune, that's for sure; and a pretty tune that's amenable to any number of arrangements, from folkie strumalong to lung-bursting soul emoting. But the real secret is in the words, what's said and not said. 'Hallelujah' alludes to so much – God, death, love, sex and music itself – without explicitly saying anything that can be pinned down. In the mould of Robbie Williams' 'Angels', it is a funeral anthem for the Noughties, an age that is secular but, you know, a little bit spiritual at the same time. In an age of media fragmentation, a song – or any work – that can appeal across generations and genres is something to be treasured.

And for what it's worth, I still reckon the Cale version is the best, but then I'm not Simon Cowell.

### Number 3: Green Day, *American Idiot* (2004)

Green Day weren't exactly what you would call critical darlings at the start of the Noughties; the best most arbiters had to say about them was that their energetic brand of pop punk wasn't quite as crass and annoying as that of, say, Blink-182. Green Day were, however, immensely popular; a state of affairs they threatened to derail entirely with the release of their 2004 album *American Idiot*.

Fans who had banged their heads since the days of singles such as 'Basket Case' might have forgiven the band for releasing a punk-rock opera with multi-part songs and recurring characters called Jesus of Suburbia and Whatsername; they might even have tolerated the message that corporate pop culture was breeding a generation of apathetic morons (including, implicitly, Green Day fans). But it was probably a bit much to expect them to absorb both blows at the same time. The critics – to their consternation – rather liked *American Idiot*, which went on to win the 2005 Grammy for Best Rock Album (and sell 14 million copies worldwide). Released 18 months after the invasion of Iraq, the album expresses the angst, anger and disillusionment many felt under the Bush administration. With America flexing its military muscle and asserting its moral rectitude, it was something of a relief to have a band doing what punks are supposed to do – expose the wound.

The title of the album may or may not have something to do with President George W Bush. Not that it mattered much, as he was re-elected a few weeks after the album was released.

## Number 2: Radiohead, *In Rainbows* (2007)

Radiohead, like Green Day, had redefined 'indie music' in the 1990s, achieving a level of commercial success and exposure that put them on a par with the biggest stadium acts – thus jeopardizing the outsider status with which indie had become associated (see also Nirvana, REM and Oasis). After 2003, however, Radiohead had become independent in the purest sense, having concluded their contract with EMI. For several years the band didn't have a recording contract. Whereas in previous eras this would have heralded commercial oblivion, in October 2007 Radiohead elected to make their seventh album available for download before it had even acquired conventional physical form.

But there was a twist; to get hold of a copy of *In Rainbows*, downloaders would have to pay – well, whatever they wanted.

This 'honesty box' system caused outrage among many music industry traditionalists, whose analysis was that Radiohead were effectively giving an album away for nothing. The fact that every Radiohead album since 2000's *Kid A* had leaked onto the internet before release (without any apparent impact on sales) didn't dissuade the doubters. This was a flawed model, they argued, and not only was it doomed to failure but it had the potential to destroy the whole music industry. Of course, when the album was released conventionally (in the last week of 2007), it topped charts on both sides of the Atlantic, picking up two Grammys in 2009.

There was an element of self-publicity to Radiohead's antics. The honesty box story might have threatened to overshadow any consideration of how good the album itself was (the critical consensus being that it offered a distinct improvement on 2003's pleasant but inessential *Hail to the Thief*), but it had implicitly laid down a challenge to the industry – stop worrying about the old model of selling music and start thinking up a new one.

### Number 1: Lily Allen, 'The Fear' (2008)

There were undoubtedly better singers than Lily Allen during the Noughties, and undoubtedly better songs than 'The Fear' (Amy Winehouse and 'Rehab' come to mind), but few that so elegantly expressed the combination of unease and emptiness that characterized the decade. Any critical response to the song is impossible to extricate from reaction to Allen herself, the privately-educated daughter of an actor and a film producer who seemed to drift into stardom as if it were a bit of a lark. Allen did little to counter this confusion, communicating via her MySpace site, where songs and self-exposure blurred seamlessly. This was the forum where 'The Fear' first saw the light of day, well before it was available to buy.

The music itself is nothing to get excited about; its loping pop sound is actually less memorable than the chirpy ska that predominated on Allen's first album. What you notice though is Allen's voice – teetering ambiguously between sneers and tears – and above all the lyrics. This is the sound of the Noughties – buying clothes, diamonds and life itself on plastic, vaguely aware of the social, environmental and economic disasters that this might provoke but not knowing or caring enough to articulate them.

'The Fear' is really just an expression of a sense of wrongness, a sense of disconnect – from morality, or even reality. The song reflects a topsy-turvy world, a world where Gordon Brown can pop up on YouTube and Iggy Pop can sell car insurance. Only in the chorus does Allen enquire, almost as an afterthought; 'When do you think it will all become clear?' She wouldn't have to wait long.

# Chapter 9

# Speaking truth to hyperpower

'To be rich is glorious.'
Deng Xiaoping

**Jai ho** (*slang; Hindi*) 'may victory be yours'[94] (2008)

In the beginning (or at least as long ago as the early 1950s) there was 'the Third World'.[95] This was as much a political definition as an economic one, referring to those nations that had not lined up (or been forced to line up) behind one or other of the post-war power blocs – that led by the United States (whose adherents became part of 'the First World') and that led by the Soviet Union (whose members comprised 'the Second World').

As the Cold War rumbled on, this definition proved increasingly inadequate as the number of non-aligned countries – those pledging fealty neither to capitalism nor communism – began to decline. 'Third World' became a catch-all term for nations that were poor, unstable and underdeveloped; countries where good governance, healthcare and education were hard to come by and the lives of citizens precarious. With many of these countries former colonies of European powers, it was perhaps not surprising that (after independence) many gravitated towards the new colonialists – the US or USSR – for financial, military and moral support. Following the Sino–Soviet split in the early 1960s, some shifted their affections to China. Many of the conflicts in the second half of the 20th century can be understood in the context of this three-way stand-off.

The collapse of Soviet communism in the late 1980s and early 1990s sent reverberations around the world. Not only did countries that had once been recipients of Moscow's *largesse* now have to fend for themselves, but Washington now saw less reason to support unsavoury regimes simply because they professed to be anti-communist (the rationale that had prompted the US to support Muslim fundamentalists in Afghanistan and Saddam Hussein in Iraq). Some isolated outposts, such as Cuba, maintained allegiance to Marxist ideology, but many of the former Soviet bloc states made the transition to capitalism; citizens often taking matters into their own hands – Berliners literally tearing down the wall that had divided their fair city for more than 20 years and the citizens of Prague precipitating the non-violent 'Velvet Revolution' in Czechoslovakia.

Still, while capitalism undoubtedly had its attractions – not least more and better goods in the shops, and the ability to travel (and work) abroad – some, particularly the older generation, mourned the old-style certainties of Five-Year Plans and jobs for life, finding the new market mentality both disconcerting and demanding. In Russia, life expectancy plummeted as levels of alcoholism continued to cause concern. When (in 2008) a TV station staged a nationwide poll to identify 'the greatest Russian', Joseph Stalin made it to third place, notwithstanding the millions who had died under his rule.

But one country had a head start in the post-Marx scramble. In 1978, Deng Xiaoping – who had become the *de facto* leader of communist China after the death of Mao Zedong – paid a visit to Singapore, the Asian city state whose combination of prosperity, cleanliness and social authoritarianism later prompted sci-fi author William Gibson to dub it 'Disneyland with the death penalty'. Always a pragmatist among the by-the-book idealists of the Chinese Communist Party, Deng saw in Singapore a model for what he would describe as 'socialism with Chinese characteristics'; essentially a capitalist economy without the distraction of political or social freedoms. In Deng's new paradigm, the Chinese were free to spend, invest and speculate, even to own. But they were still not free to question or protest. Mammon and mobiles would supplant Chairman Mao, although citizens were still expected to memorize his best sayings. In 1989, as the communist leaders of Eastern Europe were starting to see the writing on the wall, the Chinese authorities were busy suppressing student-inspired dissent in Tiananmen Square.

China had managed to avoid the worst effects of the financial crisis that had shaken east Asia in 1997, partly because its currency was pegged to the US dollar (which discouraged the worst excesses of financial speculation). When, in the late 1990s, the capitalist hothouses of Hong Kong and Macau became 'special administrative regions' of the People's Republic, there were already plenty of champagne-sipping, Porsche-driving entrepreneurs in Beijing and Shanghai; cities that, just 20 years prior, had been bastions of Mao-suited egalitarianism and conformity.

But China was not the only country to find that the Noughties represented a wave of new-found (if unequally distributed) prosperity. In the early 1990s, India had begun its transition towards a market economy, under the guidance of Finance Minister Manmohan Singh (who would become prime minister in 2004). Russia also started its transition, though it had a pretty rough ride, culminating in economic breakdown in 1998. The Noughties saw a new Russian president in the form of Vladimir Putin, who instituted a simplified tax system that promoted and encouraged growth. Over on the other side of the world, Brazil also had a rocky start to the new decade, requiring assistance from the International Monetary Fund in 2002. Still, the South American giant had soon recovered sufficiently to become an attractive location for foreign investment.

These four countries, known collectively as 'the BRIC nations' (an acronym coined in 2001 by the Goldman Sachs investment bank), between them contained well over 40% of the world's population, as well as sound infrastructure, rich natural resources and relatively stable governance. Together with the so-called 'Asian tigers' (South Korea, Taiwan, Hong Kong and Singapore) and a number of other rapidly emerging economies (among them Mexico, Indonesia and South Africa), they represented a potential challenge to the economic hegemony of North America, Western Europe and Japan.

The irony was that, to many old-world powers, the primary purpose of countries such as India and Mexico was to supply them with cheap labour and materials. Anti-capitalists protested that this was tantamount to institutionalized exploitation, a means for Western businesses to take advantage of low wages, sweatshop conditions, non-unionized workforces and lax safety regulations. Manufacturing was the first Western industry to make the move east, but many support services followed as high-speed phone and internet lines made outsourcing easier than ever. Indian call centre operators found themselves working according to London or New York time, and even having to adopt Western names.

Supporters of globalization, such as the influential economist Jeffrey Sachs, argued that it was a means of bringing investment and sound business behaviour to developing nations, and that this would ultimately be to their benefit.

What wasn't on the globalization agenda, however, was that Western businesses, if not Western workers, would take a hit, but this is exactly what happened, as Indian and Chinese companies first competed with (and then took over) Western concerns. Indian companies such as Infosys and Winpro made Bangalore a global IT hub, challenging California's Silicon Valley. In 2005, China's Lenovo took over IBM's personal computer business, while Tata of India bought the prestigious Jaguar and Land Rover vehicle brands in 2008. In a particularly symbolic move, on 2 June 2009, just one day after the 100-year-old US car giant General Motors had filed for bankruptcy, news energed that a small Chinese company called Tengzhong was in talks to pick up GM's Hummer brand, the epitome of bigger-is-better, gas-guzzling American consumerism.

Oddly, although these changes had a profound effect on the lives of people around the world, there was little evidence of them in popular culture; there would be no Noughties equivalent of the 1993 film *Rising Sun* − a slightly hysterical response to Japan's incursions into American big business. The British TV film *The Girl in the Café* (2005) touched upon issues of globalization, although it was specifically about debt relief. The closest Hollywood came to engaging with the issue was Alejandro González Iñárritu's film *Babel* (2006), the plot of which demonstrates how lives on three continents are inextricably linked, offering an analogy with the mutual responsibilities of globalized economics.

Part of the problem was this blurring of boundaries. It was easy to create conflict between an all-American hero and an Arab terrorist (as it had been with Soviet spies or Japanese businessmen). But globalization – which often relied on the movement of goods and capital through several borders and numerous hands – was not so easy to depict.

The complexities of globalization were perhaps more easily explored in books, and again publishing stepped up to the mark. Among the many books on the subject, the works of *New York Times* columnist Thomas Friedman are particularly interesting, not only because they sold in vast quantities but because they reflect changing attitudes towards a globalized world, and America's place within it. In 1999, with the Noughties clearly visible on the horizon, Friedman's *The Lexus and the Olive Tree* celebrates globalization as a process the end point of which is (essentially) universal acceptance of the American economic model. By the middle of the decade, in *The World is Flat*, globalization is not looking so benign; with the competitive playing field increasingly level, Friedman now sees it as a potential threat to the American way of life. By 2008, in *Hot, Flat and Crowded*, Friedman is even more concerned, exhorting America to take the offensive (and protect its own interests) by leading the world in the next (green) revolution.

Globalization or not, it was impossible to ignore the emergence of a new world order. Consider the seemingly endless succession of global economic conferences, and the rapidly expanding list of those who attended. Although Russia had been invited to join the economic top table with the formation of the G8 (alongside Canada, France, Germany, Italy, Japan, the UK and the US) back in 1997, it was not until 2005 that the other BRIC powers were permitted (with Mexico and South Africa) to join a grouping known as 'G8 + 5', a label that was not only unwieldy but also underlined the two-tier nature of the structure.

Although this hierarchy persisted, for example in the tradition that the International Monetary Fund should always be headed by a European and the World Bank by an American, Western powers were slowly coming round to the fact that it was ultimately unsustainable. The G20, which included representatives of the most important developing nations, had existed for much of the decade as little more than a talking shop between finance ministers and the heads of central banks. However, in November 2008, for the first time, the heads of all the G20 nations met as equals. The fact that the summit took place in Washington, DC didn't disguise the fact that the nations that had called the shots for the past couple of centuries now needed the cooperation (and in many cases the money) of countries such as China and Saudi Arabia to survive. Fittingly perhaps, Las Vegas – the global epicentre of gambling and modified reality – was to be the stage for the 2010 G20 summit.

Of course, many of these meetings were about serious matters, such as free trade, climate change and debt relief. But they were also a demonstration of power, of whose opinion counted on the world stage and whose didn't.

Despite a number of setbacks, the United States began and ended the Noughties as the world's largest economy, with the most powerful military; and although many countries objected to the invasion of Iraq and other aspects of the War on Terror, there was little they could do about it.

Nonetheless, the various failings (both moral and strategic) of US foreign policy throughout the decade, coupled with the 2008 credit crunch and ensuing economic crisis (a crisis closely associated with the free-market orthodoxies espoused by the US), meant that America had fewer friends and less influence in 2009 than it had commanded in 2000. Even the election of a new president who seemed better able to reach out beyond the physical and ideological borders of his country could not put the American Humpty back together again. America's status was suddenly precarious, that of 'default power',[96] merely maintaining its dominance until someone came up with a better offer. The gap was there to be filled.

Although the Russian bear was no longer the fearsome adversary it had been during the Cold War, its economic muscle — especially with regard to fuel — meant that few wished to annoy it. A series of disputes with the Ukraine over gas pipelines in the latter half of the Noughties caused cuts in supply to a number of EU countries, a reminder of the practical power the Russians still wielded, even without recourse to military action. The much-heralded 'Nabucco' pipeline, which promised to deliver gas to Europe bypassing Russian control, gained new impetus. Russia's heavy-handed suppression of rebellion in the breakaway republic of Chechnya at the beginning of the decade, and the South Ossetia war with Georgia in 2008, also provoked disquiet; but again, nobody took any action.

But the greatest disparity between words and action was revealed when the spotlight fell on China. As the Noughties dawned, the People's Republic had its vision of a 'Greater China' almost in place. Tibet had been annexed many years before, and efforts to eradicate indigenous culture and language through a combination of police and military force —

as well as the immigration of thousands of non-Tibetan Chinese – were well advanced. But it was show business personalities such as Richard Gere (not politicians) who took up the fight on behalf of the exiled Dalai Lama and his people, as well as pop stars such as the eccentric Icelandic singer Björk, who ruffled official feathers by calling for Tibetan independence during a concert in Shanghai. Governments tended to make their criticisms in private (or claimed to have done so). Hong Kong and Macau were once again Chinese territories, albeit enjoying more political freedom than most. Only Taiwan (to which the defeated nationalists had fled after the communists took control of mainland China in 1949) held out, much to the irritation of Beijing. The People's Republic still declared Taiwan to be an integral part of Chinese territory, and sabres were rattled at any talk of full-blown independence.

But China's influence extended further afield. One reason that the US had felt able to take action against the human rights abuses of Saddam Hussein (if that was the reason behind the invasion), but not against those that persisted in North Korea or Burma, was the extent to which China maintained interests in those countries. And it wasn't just in Asia that China had influence; it was also conspicuous in Africa, investing billions of dollars in a continent that many Western powers had effectively abandoned. Construction, mining and oil projects were beneficial to both sides, although trade agreements with such countries quickly led to a major trade deficit in the dragon's favour.

Of particular interest to the Chinese was Sudan, with its massive oil reserves. But China's involvement possibly ran deeper; there was evidence to suggest that China supplied arms to the Sudanese government for its civil war in Darfur, in direct contravention of a United Nations embargo. Once again, it was up to celebrities to fill the void left by the global political community; faded Hollywood star Mia Farrow going on hunger strike in support of victims and refugees.

Unfortunately, China was not alone in its oil-based friendships with toxic regimes. President Bush's tolerance of Saudi Arabia's human rights record was at odds with his harsh criticism of Saddam Hussein's regime in Iraq, while Condoleezza Rice's cheery welcome to President Teodoro Obiang Nguema of Equatorial Guinea in 2006 glossed over his appalling record of abuse and corruption.[97] Moreover, to point the finger at Beijing over the Sudanese situation was to expose the uncertain line between oppression and the maintenance of order; between freedom fighter and terrorist. Still, at least China's involvement in Sudan drew the world's attention to Darfur.

The attention accorded to Darfur contrasted with the inattention accorded to the Second Congo War. Despite officially ending in 2003, this terrible conflict dragged on throughout the Noughties, accounting for well over 5 million deaths (most of them occurring somewhere beyond the attention span of the Western world).

Apart from the desire not to disrupt global trade or oil supplies, there was another reason to look the other way as China bent the moral rules. The 2008 Olympics had been awarded to Beijing seven years previously, and despite assurances that human rights issues would be addressed, there was little evidence of this as the games drew near. The Hollywood director Steven Spielberg pulled out of involvement with the opening and closing ceremonies in protest over China's role in the Darfur conflict. Meanwhile, pro-Tibet activists disrupted the torch relay, prompting retaliation from tracksuited bodyguards who turned out to be from the Chinese military. The controversies did not end once the games had started.

Protestors were arrested and journalists harassed; access to the internet was restricted. The fireworks at the opening ceremony were augmented with computer graphics, while a 'singer' was revealed to have mimed to the voice of a less photogenic colleague. Serious doubts were raised about the ages of Chinese gymnasts. And yet the Beijing games were considered a major success, with new, record-smashing stars emerging in the forms of sprinter Usain Bolt and swimmer Michael Phelps.

Of course, politics have often intruded on the Olympics – in 1972, Palestinian terrorists murdered 11 Israeli athletes and coaches (events depicted in the 2005 film *Munich*); African teams walked away from the 1976 games in a dispute over apartheid and the 1980 and 1984 games were boycotted by the US and the USSR respectively. Political controversy wasn't excluded from the Beijing games, but it seemed as if most politicians thought it impolite to draw attention to its existence. The following year saw the 20th anniversary of the Tiananmen massacre, and while there was much coverage and commemoration outside China, it was all but ignored inside the country (not least because a whole generation had grown up having been told very little about it).

There was a paradox, however. While the Olympics were a massive public relations success, and the strategic and economic importance of China and the other BRIC nations was increasingly recognized, there was less progress on the cultural battleground. Every now and then an Asian or Latin American movie would achieve international success – eg *Crouching Tiger, Hidden Dragon* (Taiwan/China, 2000), *City of God* (Brazil, 2002) and *Slumdog Millionaire* (India, 2008).[98] But it was still Hollywood that dominated the cinematic landscape. We had to wait till the end of the decade for the first signs of serious potential change, Sylvester Stallone appearing with Akshay Kumar in *Kambakkht Ishq*, the first time a major Hollywood star had appeared alongside a major Indian star in a Bollywood blockbuster.

The successes of Indian cricketers (winners of the inaugural Twenty20 World Cup in 2007), Japanese baseball players (winners of the World Classic in 2006 and 2009, both on American soil) and Chinese athletes (who topped the Olympic medals table for the first time in the 2008 games) were applauded at home and abroad. Nonetheless, those who haunted the market stalls of Bangkok for bootleg sportswear were looking for Manchester United and FC Barcelona shirts, while the most popular *mitumba* (second-hand clothes) on the streets of Dar es Salaam in Tanzania declared their loyalty to the Chicago Bulls and Pittsburgh Steelers[99] (even as the Chinese government announced renewed investment in that country). The world's young still looked west; beyond Japanese manga and anime, Asian pop culture was a niche product.

To remedy this, in 2004 the Chinese government founded the Confucius Institute, which sought to create an educational centre for the dissemination of Chinese language and culture. But China still lacked the kind of global superstar who might make young people *want* to speak Chinese, rather than have to because it might help them get a job. Movie stars such as Shahrukh Khan and Zhang Ziyi were big, but they weren't Brad Pitt or Angelina Jolie; and no Asian singer had the truly cross-cultural reach of an Eminem or a Beyoncé. That said, there was at least one cultural breakthrough for the BRIC nations; in 2008, the Portuguese parliament agreed to change the spellings of hundreds of words to bring them more in line with Brazilian usage. For an approximate equivalent in the Anglosphere, it was as if the British government had decreed that the word 'colour' should be spelt without a 'u', because that's how the Americans do it.

While the developing powers' attempts to supplant Hollywood with Bollywood (or indeed Nigeria's nascent Nollywood) had achieved only moderate success by the end of the decade, they could surely have no complaints about the economic outlook. Most of the BRIC countries were recording healthy growth in GDP as the US and many Western European economies were slipping into recession.

But the idea that this was inherently a good thing was dependent on the belief that 'progress' and 'development' were always based on a model of economic expansion; where the measure of a country's wellbeing was higher output and greater material wealth. Even as China achieved the third highest net GDP in the world (overtaking Germany), other governments questioned this breakneck emulation of Western market capitalism. In Latin America, a number of political leaders – notably Hugo Chávez in Venezuela and Evo Morales in Bolivia – introduced policies that sought to prioritize equality and social justice above raw economic growth, increasing state control over key industries and utilities. Their cool relationship with the United States, and professed admiration for the Cuban model created by the ailing but still feisty Fidel Castro, provoked nervousness in US government circles; by focusing their attention on Arab jihadists, were the Americans perhaps allowing Marxist regimes to flourish in their own backyard? Fifty years before, such dissent would not have been tolerated. Now, it seemed, there was neither the will nor the means. Iraq had shown that intervention was often more trouble than it was worth.

Not that the issue was necessarily an old-style Cold War choice between communism and capitalism, however. In Asia, a number of countries developed political and economic philosophies that prioritized stability and contentment over material wealth. These included the concept of 'Gross

National Happiness' (that originated in the Himalayan kingdom of Bhutan) and the 'Sufficiency Economy' (proposed by Thailand's King Bhumibol). Critics suggested that these ideas were merely a cynical attempt by authoritarian monarchies to persuade their subjects to accept their humble lot in life; if the poor felt they had the capacity to become rich, they might agitate for more political power. At the same time, as Western economies overheated to potentially unsustainable levels (see Chapter 10), the idea of a nation having a priority other than making money felt strangely attractive to many observers.

And as the kings of Bhutan and Thailand preached the virtues of restraint and simplicity, it became apparent that the unblinking, unfettered pursuit of wealth – of second cars, second homes and second mortgages to finance the aforementioned – was not without its drawbacks.

# Chapter 10

# The bubble bursts

'Dad, you mean you're really not a superhero?'
Frédéric Beigbeder, *Windows on the World*[100]

**Bankster** (*noun*) conflation of 'banker'
and 'gangster'[101] (2008)

Throughout the Noughties, leaders such as George W Bush had a stock response to any outrage (or threat) against their country; 'These people' (a conveniently vague term for an enemy that couldn't really be defined, let alone located or defeated) would not be allowed to damage 'our [insert nation-specific adjective] way of life'.

But exactly what was that way of life; 'our' way of life? To characterize the struggle with jihadist terrorism as a Christian–Islamic conflict was counterproductive, not to mention inaccurate. Even the United States (where by some accounts over 40% of the population regularly attended church) could not be characterized as a 'Christian' nation in the same way that Iran or Pakistan could be characterized as a Muslim one. In Europe – home to many of the world's greatest churches, cathedrals and Christian artworks – people adhered to a multiplicity of faiths and belief systems, or none at all.

Instead, 'the way of life' that defined the West (and, by extension, excluded the terrorists) was a set of beliefs that most people understood, but few could identify; the product of the Renaissance and the Enlightenment, of scientific and industrial development. It was about tolerance and freedom of expression; it was about the rule of law. It was about democratic, transparent government chosen by universal adult suffrage. Binding these together was a belief in (to a greater or lesser extent) the theory and practice of free-market capitalism. The principal targets of the 9/11 attacks were not religious buildings but the Twin Towers of the World Trade Center – home to financial heavyweights such as Morgan Stanley, Lehman Brothers and Cantor Fitzgerald, not to mention (underneath 4 World Trade Center) one of the largest gold depositories in the world.

Of course, the United States and its associates had been defining themselves through the prism of capitalism well before al-Qaeda came to attention; it was what distinguished them from their communist opponents. Even Western governments that identified themselves as 'socialist', in practice simply offered a capitalist model that had a bigger role for the state, with more emphasis on material equality. By the 1980s, with the political success of Reagan and Thatcher, even this moderation fell out of fashion, and nominally leftist governments (such as those in New Zealand in the late 1980s and the UK in the late 1990s) espoused policies that gladdened the heart of many a free-market ideologue. Come the Noughties, most major economies operated on the basis that businesses – especially banks and other financial institutions – worked best when government interfered as little as possible (Adam Smith's 'invisible hand'), and that their success and prosperity benefited society as a whole. Markets were held to have an inherent rationality and stability, despite the occasional bipolar episode.

Of course, just because many governments across the world shared in this economic and political orthodoxy didn't mean that everyone else necessarily fell into line. Small groups of diehard socialists and communists – including those who had broken away from the mainstream left-wing parties – kept faith that the proletariat would come to their senses, and realize they'd been conned by the superficial glitz of consumerism. Anti-globalization protestors, meanwhile, could be relied upon to show up at any meeting involving the G8, International Monetary Fund or World Trade Organization; green hardliners sought to disrupt road and runway developments. From the other end of the argument, some of the more isolationist conservatives also began to doubt the merits of unfettered free trade, as they watched foreign interests buying up local businesses, immigration controls loosening and jobs moving abroad – concerns that also fed the paranoia of a resurgent far right.

But, for the majority of people, the intricacies of political ideology only came into play once every few years, when they came to vote. As for the intricacies of economics – inflation, budget deficits and GDP – these barely registered on the radar at all; such matters belonged in the 1970s or 80s, not the Noughties.

General understanding of the economy was based on a number of assumptions – the steady rise in house prices was a good thing, even if first-time buyers found it hard to get on the ladder; the continued availability of cheap mortgages and credit was a good thing, even if homeowners weren't sure how they were going to pay back the debt; and the eye-watering bonuses paid to the financial wizards on Wall Street and in the City of London were also a good thing, even if nobody quite knew what they were being rewarded for. Every now and then, a maverick economist or politician suggested that this state of affairs might not be sustainable (and scandals such as those at Enron and WorldCom also shook confidence), but few public figures wanted to be accused of talking down the economy; after all, the market knew best. Meanwhile, as people continued to stack up their credit and skimp on their savings, London overtook New York as the money capital of the world.[102]

Of course, when the whole thing did start to unravel, the immediate impact fell not upon stockbrokers in the City of London but upon homeowners in some of the less fashionable zip codes of the United States.

In the early years of the Noughties, some US lenders had specialized in making high-risk loans to clients with poor credit histories – the so-called 'subprime market'. This was feasible before 2004 (when interest rates stood at around 1%) but less sustainable as rates began to rise – going over 5% in 2006. Defaults and repossessions began to rise in parallel. The situation would have been bad enough if it were only the subprime specialists who had been hit; it might simply have been a rerun of the dotcom crash at the start of the decade, where damage was largely confined to one sector.

Unfortunately, it soon emerged that many of these debts had been sold on to other banks. Blue-chip names in the financial sector revealed that their exposure to the subprime market was far greater than they had previously let on. Central banks, such as the US Federal Reserve, began to cut interest rates and pump money into the ailing banking sector. The phrase 'credit crunch' – the inability or unwillingness of banks to lend to borrowers, or to each other – suddenly entered the everyday lexicon.

And then, as if the analogies with the Wall Street Crash of 1929 weren't obvious enough, there was a run on a bank. Northern Rock, a British mortgage lender with a disproportionately high exposure to subprime markets, was granted emergency support by the Bank of England. Rather than being reassured, customers swiftly withdrew around £1bn from their accounts. In February 2008, it was announced that the business was to be taken into public ownership.

This was nationalization; this was state socialism; this was not the way things were supposed to be done any more. But what was the alternative? Deregulation in the preceding years had allowed a string of mergers and acquisitions to occur, creating mega-companies that were now considered simply too big to fail, because too many other organizations would get hurt. If a company began to wobble, it might be possible to persuade another to take it on (for example, JP Morgan's acquisition of the 85-year-old Bear Stearns in March 2008 and Bank of America's takeover of Merrill Lynch in September of the same year). But this was just a way of creating even bigger organizations that had even less latitude for failure.

So, it seemed preferable to keep companies separate, offering financial support and guarantees to those that were suffering. But this could just be seen as chucking good money (if there was such a thing any more) after bad. The banks were failing because of the behaviour of bankers who still remained in control; the only difference now was that the money they had to play with came not from diabolically complex financial instruments – derivatives, hedge funds and securities – but from the public purse. Wouldn't it be better to get rid of the bankers who caused the problem, and let government take over the helm?

Sometimes this wasn't feasible, as whole countries suffered from the downturn; Iceland and Hungary teetering close to bankruptcy. But other governments, although down, were by no means out. So why was there reluctance to use the takeover option more widely? Because that would be an admission too far, as the writer John Lanchester noted:

> There is, however, a deeper embarrassment, one which verges on a form of psychological or ideological crisis. To nationalize major financial institutions would mean that the Anglo-Saxon model of capitalism had failed. The level of state intervention in the UK and US at this moment is comparable to that of wartime. We have in effect had to declare war to get us out of the hole created by our economic system. There is no model or precedent for this, and no way to argue that it's all right really, because under such-and-such a model of capitalism...there is no such model. It just isn't supposed to work like this, and there is no road-map for what's happened.[103]

Sometimes it was possible to smudge the distinction between nationalization and subsidy by setting conditions for financial support. When the British government made a multi-billion-pound donation to the Royal Bank of Scotland (in terms of asset size, the largest company in the world), it might have been a good moment to suggest a little public humility on the part of those who had brought it to the brink of ruin. But that seemed to be more easily said than done. The outgoing Chairman, Sir Fred Goodwin, was able to claim a hefty pension for the rest of his life, and there was little the government could do about it, even though (as one Cabinet minister put it) the pay-out was unacceptable 'in the court of public opinion'. Goodwin later accepted a cut in his pension, but this was perhaps more expediency than morality.

Of course, Goodwin was not the only offender. Across the Atlantic, high-flying financier Bernard Madoff was arrested after having confessed to defrauding investors of $50bn in an elaborate global Ponzi scheme. The undoubted drama of Madoff's story – he was ultimately turned in by his two sons, having admitted his business was 'all just one big lie' – only added a seedy glamour to the whole affair, as did details of some of the investors he had duped, including Hollywood director Steven Spielberg.

But was Madoff in some way an easy target? Yes, he had crossed the line in the most spectacular fashion, but what about those who had encouraged or presided over the environment in which he operated? In October 2008, Alan Greenspan, the former Chairman of the Federal Reserve (and champion of unfettered free-market capitalism), told the House Committee on Oversight and Government Reform; '[I found a] flaw in the model'. Back in the UK, Sir John Gieve, Deputy Governor of the Bank of England, admitted that the Bank had underestimated the severity of the financial situation; 'crazy borrowing' was taking place and the prices of houses and other assets were rising unsustainably but, according to Gieve, the Bank had not fully understood the problem.

But were the greedy bankers solely to blame for the situation, or were we – the consumer, the homeowner, the debtor – also partly at fault, because we believed them, or wanted to believe them? After all, as long as house prices kept going up...

Wherever the blame truly lay, heroes as well as villains emerged from the crisis. The TV host Jon Stewart had built up a unique role in American media; a combination of stand-up comedian and news anchor. It was widely reported that, for a good proportion of the under-30s, Stewart's *Daily Show* was the primary source of information on current affairs. Still, however biting Stewart's satire, it tended to be overlaid with a detached sense of irony; until, that is, the iniquities of the credit crunch pushed him into the role of righteous avenger.

In March 2009, Stewart's public excoriation of stock market analyst Jim Cramer became a viral sensation as he accused the CNBC star of encouraging the sort of short-termism that had provoked the financial crisis; talking up stocks such as Bear Sterns even as they were going down the drain. Cramer was prepared to admit particular errors of judgement, but Stewart's indignation cut to the heart of the matter; 'I think the difference is not good call/bad call' he argued. 'The difference is real market and unreal market.' The fact that it was left to a comedian to offer the clearest analysis of the situation ('Wow! He runs a variety show' Cramer had sneered when Stewart had first singled him out) spoke volumes.[104]

But for all the plaudits Stewart earned for his skewering of Cramer, he *did* only run a variety show, and as such all he could really do was shrug in an amusing manner; governments and central banks had more momentous responsibilities. The Federal Reserve had been forced into the role of economic triage station, deciding which institutions deserved saving and which should be left to their fate. In early September 2008, the Reserve was faced with such a choice – bail out the mortgage lenders Fannie Mae and Freddie Mac, and take an 80% stake in the insurance giant AIG (the definitive 'too big to fail' entity), but allow the 158-year-old investment bank Lehman Brothers (which had just posted a quarterly loss of $3.9bn) to collapse. They chose the latter; Lehman filing for bankruptcy on 15 September.

The bankruptcy of Lehman Brothers was a grim reminder that – in the real world – banks do fail, and such failures are as much a part of capitalism as bespoke suits and bonuses.

Many people, however, refused to accept this reality and were infuriated at the prospect of banks receiving state handouts, especially those that had seemingly brought things on themselves by dabbling in what amounted to fiscal metaphysics. As Neil Young sang on his 2009 album *Fork in the Road*; 'There's a bailout coming, but it's not for you, it's for all those creeps hiding what they do.'

On September 29, Congress debated and rejected a massive government bailout package for Wall Street banks. Every single company on Standard & Poor's 500 Index lost value as a result, with one exception – the Campbell Soup Company. Clearly, what the world needed was not a chain of deals so complex that nobody was quite able to digest them. What was needed was something plain and simple; cream of mushroom rather than collateralized debt obligation or credit default swap. Or maybe it was just that there was little else we could afford. All we could do now was hunker down and eat our soup – cold, if Russia decided to turn off the gas.

'Stuff', as the US Defense Secretary Donald Rumsfeld had famously remarked when discussing looting in Baghdad, still went on happening.[105] In the midst of all this financial turmoil, the dashing Barack Obama swept into power in the United States on a tidal wave of goodwill, hope and online donations. Obama was a breath of fresh air, re-engaging the interest of young people in politics and going some way towards repairing the racial faultlines that had riven his country since its founding. Once in office, however, Obama inevitably antagonized his opponents and disappointed his supporters. But he bought a puppy and announced the closure of Guantánamo. He took his wife Michelle to a Broadway show and proposed healthcare reforms. He stretched out a hand to the Muslim world and travelled to Europe, where Michelle dazzled the press and hugged the Queen of England. Was there perhaps a new Camelot on the horizon?

But something had changed. Although the credit crunch had confirmed the centrality of the United States in global economics ('If America sneezes, the whole world catches cold'), it had also demonstrated the fallibility of the financial system upon which it relied. Business writers and trainers had long asserted that the Chinese word for crisis was a combination of 'danger' and 'opportunity'; in linguistic terms, this wasn't quite true, but there were a few valiant entrepreneurs who couldn't stop believing.

Meanwhile, in June 2009, Kiva, a San Francisco-based non-profit organization that coordinated microfinance payments to enterprises in the developing world, announced that it was considering offering its services to deserving clients in the United States. For some in the West, it seemed that everything we had tried to protect – our jobs, our homes, our security – was under threat.

As reports of capitalism's death filled the air, many argued for a more sustainable, low-carbon economic model. As the author (and Policy Director of the New Economics Foundation) Andrew Simms put it; 'Instead of scrabbling to return the economy to business as usual, this could be our last chance to save the economy and prevent environmental bankruptcy.' But for governments staring the prospect of recession (if not depression) in the face, the immediate priority was to shore up what we had. Later – as some detected the first faint signs of economic stabilization and others rushed to protect their interests – proposals to tighten up financial regulation and oversight fell short of expectation.

As countries around the world slipped into varying degrees of financial gloom, publishers rushed to throw some light on the situation. New editions were hurriedly put to press, while seminal works such as JK Galbraith's *The Great Crash of 1929* (originally published back in 1954) gained new momentum. Galbraith was soon joined by other big hitters such as the speculative financier George Soros and the Nobel Prize winner Paul Krugman; the latter's *The Return of Depression Economics and the Crisis of 2008* was not the only title to remind us that we had been here before. Fiction also had its say, with Margaret Atwood once again on the money; her incisive collection of essays on the role of debt in our lives and culture, *Payback*, published as many of us heard the knock at the door. Sebastian Faulks' novel *A Week in December* (2009) also caught the *zeitgeist*.

Others in the wider artistic community were also on the scent. The British director Dominic Savage was already working on his TV film *Freefall* (which follows the intertwined stories of a banker, mortgage salesman and hapless mortgagee), though sometimes he found real-life events running ahead of plotlines.[106] Meanwhile, over in the US, Michael Moore began work on a film about Wall Street corruption.

If we believe (with Ferdinand Mount – see Introduction) that 'decaditis' is a nonsense, and that the Noughties really began on September 11, 2001, then they ended almost exactly seven years later, on September 15, 2008, with the fall of

Lehman Brothers. And, of course, the Noughties ended in exactly the same place they had begun – a place where two proud towers had once stood; a place where 'Masters of the Universe'[107] (like the bankers at Lehmans) had once plied their lucrative trade.

The destruction of the World Trade Center and the fall of Lehman Brothers were both, in a sense, the result of a fundamental disconnection from reality; of a fanatical trust in the rightness of an ideology on the one hand and an unquestioning belief in the rectitude of the market on the other. Of course, it would be preposterous to suggest that the events at Lehmans were in any way in the same league as those of 9/11; nonetheless, for some, they did both speak of destructive delusion.

Meanwhile, in November 2006, work began on Daniel Libeskind's 'Freedom Tower' at Ground Zero. All over New York City, people looked on in hope and disbelief. Bankers, lawyers, cleaners, tramps.

# Conclusion – Predicting the present

> 'Time past and time future
> What might have been and what has been
> Point to one end, which is always present.'
> TS Eliot, 'Burnt Norton'[108]

**Ringxiety** (*noun*) the confusion experienced by a group of people when a cell or mobile phone rings and no one is sure whose phone it is (2004)

Around the time I started writing this book, I picked up another; a second-hand copy of *Our Future: Dr Magnus Pyke predicts*, a paperback from 1980. In this book, the eccentric Dr Pyke (a well-known figure on British television in the 1970s)[109] muses on what life might be like in 50 years' time. Since we are now more than halfway towards 2030, we can take a pretty good view on how accurate (or not) his predictions were.

Sometimes Dr Pyke was magnificently right (internet grocery shopping), and sometimes he was quite magnificently wrong (washable nylon newspapers). But that doesn't really matter; such prognostication is really little more than erudite guesswork, and inevitably says more about the time in which the predictions were made than it does about any nominal target date. More recent bouts of futurological 'what-iffery', such as Bruce Sterling's *Tomorrow Now* (which also looks forward 50 years, but has 2003 as its start date), will doubtless seem quaint and/or hilarious in two or three decades' time; they are really about the Noughties, not the 2050s.[110]

So, it would be tempting fate surely if I were to conclude with some speculation about how the next decade (whatever it is to be called – 'the tens', 'the teens', 'the twenty tens'?) might pan out? After all, prediction is a highly unpredictable science. Still, I am not above temptation.

President Chelsea Clinton will win the Nobel Peace Prize for averting war between Columbia and Venezuela; Richard Branson will launch the first solar-powered transatlantic airliner and Russell Crowe will become the supreme ruler of the United Republic of the Antipodes. Madonna and Angelina Jolie will adopt each other's children, by mistake.

More plausibly, we may well see a two-state solution to the Israel–Palestine problem bring an edgy peace, at least for a while. We may also see Britain leaving the European Union, a major mammal species becoming extinct in the wild and a fully 3D, CGI creation winning the Oscar for Best Picture. We may perhaps see someone running a marathon in under two hours, although the realization (after the debacle of the 2016 Olympics) that drug tests are a hopeless gesture will mean few people will really care.

On the other hand – as Magnus Pyke and Bruce Sterling would no doubt agree – we may not. But this book isn't about the future. This is a book about the past, albeit (as I write) a past so recent that the edges bleed imperceptibly into nowness without us being able to distinguish the difference. So I have no excuse, have I? I'm not making wild guesses about the 2050s; I'm looking backwards, from the relative comfort of the future.

But even this has its complications. Critics will say that I am simply too close to discern any meaningful patterns or perceptions – even to distinguish a few common threads – in this period of time we have called 'the Noughties'. (And there is always the danger of some major event coming up and biting me before the decade is officially through.) But maybe now is a good time to reflect, while we can still remember the sights, sounds and nuances of this mixed-up kid of a decade. Maybe now is the perfect time to identify a few common threads.

In his exceedingly short story 'On Exactitude in Science',[111] the Argentinean author Jorge Luis Borges explored the idea of mythical cartographers who were never satisfied with the detail of their maps until they had drawn one that was exactly the same size as the area it depicted. Using the same logic, to depict 10 years in 1:1 scale would take a further 10 years, rather than the couple of hundred pages I have at my disposal.

I trust that there is very little in this book that is actually wrong *per se*, but you may well feel that there are sins of omission, if not commission. Maybe you wanted more about the theatre or fashion than I have included, or perhaps you felt the lack of an in-depth analysis of the rivalry between Pakistan and India over the disputed territory of Kashmir. Maybe you yearned for a discussion about whether Nicole Scherzinger should or shouldn't leave the Pussycat Dolls. Perhaps you detected a political or philosophical bias, or a tendency to overuse footnotes.[112] But, as the Hollywood producer Robert Evans said in the 2002 documentary *The Kid Stays in the Picture* (one of the many films of the decade that I might have mentioned in Chapter 4, but didn't); 'There are three sides to every story – yours, mine and the truth. No one is lying. Memories shared serve each other differently.'

But this conclusion isn't simply a pre-emptive apology for the fact that my truth isn't necessarily yours. It reflects back on a key theme of the book – the nature of reality and unreality; the understanding of 'truth'.

America's 'innocence' was not the only concept to have perished in the 9/11 attacks, the fragile triumph of rational Enlightenment thought that the American political economist Francis Fukuyama had trumpeted in 1992 also met an untimely death (although, admittedly, it had been in poor health for some time). In the United States, educated, reasonable people were arguing that God had indeed created the world in six days, about 6,000 years previously. Meanwhile, in China, other educated people were making equally cogent arguments that social and political freedoms were unnecessary distractions from the overriding necessity of economic self-determination. These were all 'truths', all realities; the idea that flying an airplane into a skyscraper might in some way be a good thing to do was just another example, albeit one that made for more exciting news bulletins.

Everyone seemed to be at it. Politicians realized that things just needed to sound right, not necessarily *be* right. In response to all this chatter, comedian Stephen Colbert coined the term 'truthiness', meaning the quality of stating concepts or facts one wishes or believes to be true, rather than those known to be true. Colbert only came up with the word in 2005, but it seems unlikely that George W Bush would have been able to sell the Iraq invasion to the American people without it.

One of the things we learned in the Noughties is that nothing – not global capitalism, not military intervention, not Wikipedia,

Facebook or Twitter – will force people to stop believing their own fundamental truths, or even truthinesses. I realized this early in the decade, as I stood at a roadside stall in Bangkok, the first night I spent in the city. Looking up the street, I saw a 7-Eleven convenience store, then another. In the opposite direction, I made out the familiar features of Colonel Sanders. Filled with anti-globalization, anti-branding self-righteousness (the flames doubtless fanned by several readings of Naomi Klein and Kalle Lasn), I grumbled that this could be any big city – Barcelona, Buenos Aires, Bangalore. Then an elephant tapped me on the shoulder. America Is Not The World, as Morrissey had warbled back in 2004, but by the end of the decade this had become a fact rather than a warning or a protest.

And this wasn't just a matter of different truths separating different countries or cultures. In his bestselling book *The Long Tail* (2006), Chris Anderson (Editor-in-Chief of *Wired* magazine) drew attention to the high proportion of Amazon book sales that derived from less popular titles. This reflected not simply the huge inventory that the online retailer was able to offer in comparison with a conventional, bricks-and-mortar bookshop, but also the fragmentation and diversification of culture and taste.

Of course, the educated have always fretted about the tastes of the semi-educated; a concern that predates even the anti-Gutenberg grumbles of Hieronimo Squarciafico. This same issue also caused considerable anxiety to Victorians such as Matthew Arnold and Edmund Gosse, who predicted that universal free education would provoke a democratization of taste and, as a result, a state of 'irreparable chaos'. Throughout the 20th century, what could be described as 'high culture' – serious literature, fine art and classical music – was pushed inexorably to the fringes of public discourse, where it made the acquaintance of hard science. The Western canon was as dead as the White Males who notoriously peopled it – Plato, Leonardo, Shakespeare, Voltaire, Mozart, Kant, Darwin, Marx, Arnold and Gosse. But the old canon was replaced not by chaos but by a new and slightly more accessible version of itself, this time determined by popularity – the chart-topping record, the top-rating TV show. From the perspective of the Dead White Males and their ageing fan club, the lunatics had taken over the asylum, but at least someone was still making choices; at least someone, somewhere, was still in charge.

Gosse's nightmare only became a reality in the Noughties, when even this populist interpretation of culture began to dissolve. The idea of whole families gathering around the same TV set or teenagers listening to a definitive pop chart seemed almost absurd. This lack of focus not only had an effect on the producers of culture – who found themselves addressing increasingly narrow and diffuse demographic segments – but also on wider society. Politicians, journalists and comedians could no longer rely on their audiences picking up cultural references; a moderately amusing one-liner about quantitative easing or Flight of the Conchords could die a death simply because most folk didn't know what you were talking about.

As far back as Chapter 6, I noted that two of the defining themes of the Noughties were technology and fear; but perhaps the decade really came into its own at the places where these two intersected – fear of technology, the technology of fear, fear of fear and so on. Never before had humanity had such an opportunity for knowledge and information, for education and understanding – the combined wisdom of centuries at the tap of a finger. But, in the Noughties, the rules of engagement had irrevocably changed. At the start of the decade, we were still sitting down in front of a personal computer or TV screen (or maybe even a book, paper or magazine) to receive information. By the end of the decade, however, information was moving seamlessly between PC and BlackBerry, between iTunes, iPhone and iPod, and we accessed it standing up and lying down as much as sitting. What is more, we were no longer passive recipients; we actively tweeted, poked, texted, messaged and blogged. We took issue with stuffy newspaper columnists and, when they didn't respond, added scurrilous notes to their Wikipedia entries.

And yet we were seemingly overwhelmed by the responsibility, by the sheer volume of data at our disposal. We took advice from Amazon that if we liked book 'X' we might like 'Y', but there didn't seem to be much scope for finding that offbeat choice, 'Z'. Rather than picking fights, we gravitated towards opinions that reflected our own prejudices; pro- or anti-Israel, pro- or anti-animal testing. 'Too much information!' we responded when someone tweeted an intimate detail; and the more information there was, the less we absorbed – either it bored us, confused us or we simply didn't want to know. The Noughties had the potential to become a digital version of Plato's *Symposium*; instead, they were more like the Tower of Babel.[113]

But there was a paradox at work here. Despite all these fantastic changes, our world was still not particularly fantastical. The sci-fi future we had half-expected to wake up to on the morning of January 1, 2000 had simply not materialized. Notwithstanding the imaginings of Magnus Pyke and Bruce Sterling, most of us still travelled to work by car or train (not jetpack), consumed peaches and pork chops (not protein pills) and had sweaty sex (not cybersex).

Look at a group photo in a family home from 1960, and then one from 1969, and the differences – from haircuts to soft furnishings – will be immense. Now look at one from

2000, then one from 2009. Give or take a new plasma-screen TV, there's not much in it. But we know that so much happened between those two photos being taken; and not simply that one of them could now be uploaded to Flickr. The War on Terror, climate change and economic collapse made for a tumultuous and, in many ways, a frightening decade. Advances in technology also meant that we could witness these convulsions in greater detail than ever before.

So, what happened when these two themes – technology and fear – collided? They tore each other apart. Yes, of course, in many ways technological innovation offered us unprecedented freedoms; but there always seemed to be a downside. This was the decade you could purchase almost anything from the security of your own home, but have your identity and money stolen without anyone setting foot inside your door. This was the decade you could access almost any information, but so too could potential terrorists. This was the decade you could voice your views to millions, but so too could the unhinged. This was the decade you could feel safe on the streets, until CCTV picked you up for littering.

Yes, of course, you could also have a great deal fun; this, after all, was the decade you could tweet Tony Blair, poke Paris Hilton or film yourself on YouTube. This was the decade you could mess around with endless friends (even though you might never meet them) or disrupt traditional business models with the click of a mouse. But, in some ways, the Noughties just weren't naughty enough – there was always someone watching, always someone feeling fearful.

There was another paradox at the heart of the Noughties. Everything had changed, but in a sense the change was nothing;

not no change as such, but a tangible absence. So many of the decade's important events and cultural markers were defined by their non-existence. The Noughties began with the celebration of a millennium that, in strictly chronological terms, hadn't yet started. The most powerful man on Earth, George W Bush, achieved his position thanks to the painstaking enumeration of holes (absences of paper) on election slips, while his mortal enemy was someone who existed only in blurred sound and vision. Meanwhile, the supreme folly of Bush's presidency was predicated on the existence of weapons that never were. Similarly, just as most people in the world hadn't heard of the World Trade Center until after it had disappeared, fewer still knew of a bank called Lehman Brothers until it filed for bankruptcy, exposing the inherent fallibility of Jon Stewart's 'unreal markets'.

In the arts, the decade kicked off with the alleged suicide of 'Luther Blissett' (a joint identity for political activists and artists), even though he'd never been alive.[114] The musician Danger Mouse threatened to release a blank CD, while the author Jim Crace – thanks to a misunderstanding somewhere between his publisher and Amazon – discovered he had inadvertently written a book that didn't exist, when a misreading of a preliminary title for a work-in-progress mysteriously acquired a publication date, page count, price and ISBN.[115] Meanwhile, over in New York, the 9/11 memorial was named 'Reflecting Absence'.

Time and again, the Noughties spoke of paradox and duality. But maybe this was the point; maybe this was why the decade was so significant, why it did finally make a name for itself. Maybe this natural awkwardness, this confusion of fear and technology, of connection and disconnection, reality and unreality, really was the shape of the future.

# New beginnings

A selective list of novel words and phrases we gained (or which came to prominence) in the Noughties:

## 2000

**Bling** (*noun, adjective*) ostentatious jewellery, especially as worn by hip-hop devotees

**Crackberry** (*noun*) BlackBerry personal computer, or someone who uses it compulsively

**Doomsdate** (*noun*) date upon which technological malfunction will occur, eg Y2K or the predicted activation of a computer virus or worm

**Fo' shizzle** (*slang*) for sure, as used in Snoop Dogg's 'What's My Name (Pt 2)'

**Hanging chad** (*noun*) incompletely punched hole; with specific reference to contentious ballots cast at the 2000 US presidential election

**Spyware** (*noun*) software installed on a computer to collect information without the user's consent

## 2001

**9/11** (*noun*) events surrounding the attacks on the World Trade Center and the Pentagon on September 11, 2001 as well as the aborted attack presumed to have been intended for Washington, DC

**Bastard pop** (*noun*) a composition created by blending two or more musical pieces into a single work, usually without the permission of the copyright holder

**Impeachment nostalgia** (*noun*) a longing for the superficial news of the Clinton era

**Islamofascism** (*noun*) political ideas ascribed by opponents to Islamic fundamentalists and extremists

**Password fatigue** (*noun*) inability to remember multiple passwords, PIN numbers etc

**Weapon of mass destruction** (*noun*) device (especially nuclear, chemical or biological) that can cause massive and widespread destruction of people, structures and environment

## 2002

**Enronomics** (*noun*) business strategy based on illegal or unethical accounting practices

**Leisure sickness** (*noun*) the phenomenon of people (especially workaholics) being more likely to feel ill during vacations and weekends than on work days

**NASCAR dad** (*noun*) American, white, working-class father; usually in the context of political demographics

**Noob (or n00b)** (*noun*) newcomer to an online activity who fails to learn from their mistakes

**Pre-emptive self-defence** (*noun*) an attack before a possible attack

**Regime change** (*noun*) euphemism for the enforced removal of a government or leader; with specific reference to Saddam Hussein

## 2003

**Freedom fries** (*noun*) euphemism for French fries, coined by Republican congressmen as a protest against France's opposition to the Iraq war

**Manscaping** (*noun*) intimate male grooming

**Meh** (*adjective*) uninspiring, mediocre

**Metrosexual** (*noun, adjective*) fashion-conscious, well-groomed heterosexual male

**Nicotini** (*noun*) cocktail containing tobacco juice (to bypass smoking bans)

**Sex up** (*verb*) to impose spin on a document or presentation; gained currency when applied to 'the September dossier', the UK government's documents on events leading to the Iraq War

**Twunt** (*noun; vulgar*) idiot

## 2004

**Chav** (*noun*) pejorative term for young, white, poorly-educated, working-class Briton

**Garriage** (*noun*) gay marriage or civil partnership

**Ringxiety** (*noun*) the confusion experienced by a group of people when a cell or mobile phone rings and no one is sure whose phone it is

**Snowclone** (*noun*) overused phrasal template (eg 'X is the new Y'; 'weapons of mass X')

**Totty shot** (*noun*) inessential image of an attractive woman, used to attract the male viewer/reader (eg photographs of pretty teenagers celebrating examination results)

**Wardrobe malfunction** (*noun*) euphemism for accidental exposure of flesh; from the uncovering of Janet Jackson's nipple at the 2004 Super Bowl

## 2005

**Blook** (*noun*) a book based on content that originated as a blog

**Extraordinary rendition** (*noun*) the surrendering of a suspect or detainee to another jurisdiction, especially overseas

**Jump the couch** (*verb*) to exhibit frenetic behaviour, from Tom Cruise's bizarre expression of love for Katie Holmes on *The Oprah Winfrey Show*

**Lifehack** (*noun, verb*) a tool or technique to make one's life easier

**Playlist anxiety** (*noun*) concern about what other people might think of the music on one's iPod or other digital music-player

**Sexting** (*verb*) sending sexually explicit material by mobile or cell phone

**Truthiness** (*noun*) that which we want or believe to be true, independent of factual evidence; popularized by the comedian Stephen Colbert

## 2006

**Decaditis** (*noun*) the fallacy that 'slicing the past up into periods of 10 years [is] a useful thing to do'

**Flog** (*noun*) a commercial website disguised as a personal blog

**Make it rain** (*verb*) to throw banknotes at a crowd of people in order to demonstrate affluence; widely popularized by the Fat Joe single of the same name

**Mankini** (*noun*) sling bathing costume worn by men; popularized in the film *Borat: Cultural learnings of America for make benefit glorious nation of Kazakhstan*

**Plutoed** (*adjective*) demoted or devalued; a reference to Pluto losing its planetary status

**Pwn** (*verb*) to defeat or best another person, usually in an online context

**Slow blogging** (*noun*) an ideology that supports irregular, considered blog posts over short, immediate responses

**Wii elbow** (*noun*) pain or numbness resulting from excessive use of the Wii

## 2007

**Celebutard** (*noun*) a stupid celebrity

**Copyrighteous** (*adjective*) the quality of being smug over one's adherence to intellectual property regulations

**Global weirding** (*noun*) an increase in unusual environmental activity, often attributed to climate change

**Googlegänger** (*noun*) someone with the same name as you, found through self-Googling

**Locavore** (*noun*) someone who eats only (or mainly) food that is produced locally

**Peternity leave** (*noun*) time off to bond with a new pet, or care for a sick one

**Subprime** (*adjective*) used to describe a loan or mortgage with high risk, usually because of the client's poor or non-existent credit record

## 2008

**Authenticitude** (*noun*) the appropriation of cutting-edge street trends (eg skateboarding) by commercial concerns

**Bailout** (*noun*) the rescue by government of companies on the brink of collapse, especially large banks and financial institutions

**Bankster** (*noun*) conflation of 'banker' and 'gangster'

**Bromance** (*noun*) intense, non-sexual relationship between two straight men

**Cultural scentlessness** (*noun*) the quality of being equally accessible to people from many different cultures (originally with reference to the characters of the Japanese author Haruki Murakami)

**Jai ho** (*slang; Hindi*) 'may victory be yours'; as popularized in the film *Slumdog Millionaire*

**Mindcasting** (*noun*) an activity that involves sending message posts (eg on Twitter) about what one is thinking rather than what one is doing

**Terrorist fist jab** (*noun*) knuckle-to-knuckle greeting, as performed by Barack and Michelle Obama at a rally in Minnesota; given sinister connotations by conservative media commentators

**Truman Show syndrome** (*noun*) mental condition whereby sufferers believe they are participants in a reality TV show; a reference to the 1998 film starring Jim Carrey

**Twibe** (*noun*) group of Twitter users with a common interest

## 2009

**Funemployment** (*noun*) the phenomenon of enjoyable periods of unemployment, often cushioned by generous severance payments

**Prosthetic knowledge** (*noun*) information that a person does not know, but knows they can access immediately via technology

**Terafy** (*verb*) to instil fear by mentioning the US trillion-dollar budget deficit

**Unplandlord** (*noun*) someone forced by economic conditions to rent out a property rather than sell it

**Weisure** (*noun*) free time spent on work-related activities

**Zombie bank** (*noun*) a financial institution that only survives because of government support, usually because it is regarded as being 'too big to fail'

*Acknowledgement is due to the American Dialect Society, the Global Language Monitor, urbandictionary.com, Wiktionary, wordnik.com and wordspy.com.*

# Endings

A selective list of people, concepts and cultural landmarks we lost in the Noughties:

## 2000

'Luther Blissett', writer, activist
Barbara Cartland, writer
Alex Comfort, writer, doctor
Ian Dury, musician
John Gielgud, actor
Alec Guinness, actor
Screamin' Jay Hawkins, musician
Reggie Kray, gangster
Kirsty MacColl, musician
Charles Schulz, cartoonist
Pops Staples, musician
Pierre Trudeau, politician

Don Bradman, cricketer
John Diamond, journalist
Carlo Giuliani, activist
George Harrison, musician
John Lee Hooker, musician
Tove Jansson, writer
Ken Kesey, writer
Timothy McVeigh, Oklahoma City bomber
privacy
Joey Ramone, musician
WG Sebald, writer
Charles Trenet, musician
Auberon Waugh, journalist
Webvan, online grocer
The World Trade Center

## 2001

Aaliyah, musician
Douglas Adams, writer
Balthus, painter

## 2002

Milton Berle, comedian
Pierre Bourdieu, sociologist
Lonnie Donegan, musician
Pim Fortuyn, politician

John Gotti, mafia boss
Stephen Jay Gould, writer,
    evolutionary biologist
Richard Harris, actor
Harry Hay, activist
Thor Heyerdahl, explorer
Myra Hindley, Moors murderer
Jam-Master Jay, DJ
Waylon Jennings, musician
Chuck Jones, animator
Peggy Lee, musician
Alan Lomax, musicologist
Lisa 'Left Eye' Lopes, musician
Linda Lovelace, actor
Spike Milligan, comedian
Daniel Pearl, journalist
Joe Strummer, musician
Stanley Unwin, comedian
Billy Wilder, film director

**2003**

Idi Amin, military ruler
Hank Ballard, musician
Luciano Berio, composer
Maurice Blanchot,
    philosopher
Roberto Bolaño, writer
Charles Bronson, actor
Johnny and June Carter Cash,
    musicians
Leslie Cheung, actor
Madame Chiang Kai-shek,
    political spouse

The Columbia space shuttle
    crew
Leopoldo Galtieri, military
    ruler
Althea Gibson, tennis player
Katharine Hepburn, actor
Thora Hird, actor
Bob Hope, comedian
Qusay and Uday Hussein,
    sons of Saddam Hussein
David Kelly, weapons expert
Sam Phillips, record producer
Leni Riefenstahl, film director
    and propagandist
Fred Rogers, TV host
Edward Said, writer, academic
Slim Dusty, musician
Elliott Smith, musician
William Steig, cartoonist
Denis Thatcher, businessman,
    political spouse
Strom Thurmond, politician
Timothy Treadwell,
    environmentalist
Barry White, musician
Sheb Wooley, actor, musician

**2004**

Yasser Arafat, Palestinian
    leader
Marlon Brando, actor
Henri Cartier-Bresson,
    photographer

Ray Charles, musician
Francis Crick, molecular
    biologist
Jacques Derrida, philosopher
*The Face*, magazine
Paul Foot, journalist, activist
Rick James, musician
Estée Lauder, businesswoman
Janet Leigh, actor
Norris McWhirter, editor,
    activist
Russ Meyer, film director
Jeff Nuttall, writer, artist
Ol' Dirty Bastard, musician
John Peel, DJ
Fernando Poe Jr, actor,
    politician
Tony Randall, actor
Ronald Reagan, actor,
    politician
Christopher Reeve, actor,
    activist
Hubert Selby Jr, writer
Susan Sontag, writer, activist
Peter Ustinov, writer, actor
Theo van Gogh, film director
Fay Wray, actor

## 2005

Ronnie Barker, actor
Saul Bellow, writer
Peter Benenson, lawyer,
    activist

George Best, footballer
Johnny Carson, TV host
Johnnie Cochran, lawyer
Robin Cook, politician
Andrea Dworkin, writer,
    activist
King Fahd of Saudi Arabia
Frank Gorshin, actor
Rafik Hariri, politician
Pope John Paul II
Philip Johnson, architect
Jean Charles de Menezes,
    mistaken for suicide
    bomber
Arthur Miller, writer
Mo Mowlam, politician
Kerry Packer, businessman
Richard Pryor, comedian
Terri Schiavo, medical *cause
    célèbre*
Hunter S Thompson, writer
Luther Vandross, musician
Simon Wiesenthal, Nazi
    hunter
*Zembla*, magazine

## 2006

Robert Altman, film director
Syd Barrett, musician
Oriana Fallaci, journalist
Betty Friedan, writer, activist
Milton Friedman, economist
JK Galbraith, economist,
    diplomat

Heinrich Harrer, mountaineer
Charles Haughey, politician
Nasreen Huq, activist
Saddam Hussein, military
  ruler
Steve Irwin, environmentalist
Coretta Scott King, activist
Arthur Lee, musician
Alexander Litvinenko, former
  security agent
Slobodan Miloševic,
  politician
Moose, canine actor
Wilson Pickett, musician
Augusto Pinochet, military
  ruler
Anna Politkovskaya,
  journalist
Elisabeth Schwarzkopf,
  musician
*Smash Hits*, magazine
Linda Smith, comedian
Aaron Spelling, TV producer
Mickey Spillane, writer
*Top of the Pops*, TV show
Jack Wild, actor

## 2007

Momofuku Ando, inventor
Michelangelo Antonioni, film
  director
Jean Baudrillard, philosopher

Ingmar Bergman, film
  director
Benazir Bhutto, politician
Sri Chinmoy, guru
Alice Coltrane, musician
Alan Coren, writer, satirist
WF Deedes, journalist,
  politician
Hrant Dink, journalist
Jerry Falwell, evangelist
Ryszard Kapuscinski,
  journalist
Evel Knievel, motorcycle
  daredevil
Verity Lambert, TV producer
Norman Mailer, writer
Marcel Marceau, mime
  artist
Arthur Marshall, aviation
  engineer
George Melly, writer,
  musician
Tammy Faye Messner,
  evangelist
Luciano Pavarotti, operatic
  tenor
Abbé Pierre, priest
Max Roach, musician
Anita Roddick,
  businesswoman, activist
Mstislav Rostropovich,
  musician

Anna Nicole Smith, model
*The Sopranos*, TV show
Karlheinz Stockhausen,
    composer
Paul Tibbets, pilot
Ike Turner, musician
Chad Varah, priest,
    campaigner
Kurt Vonnegut, writer
Robert Anton Wilson, writer
Tony Wilson, businessman,
    journalist

**2008**

Richard Blackwell, fashion
    critic
William F Buckley Jr, writer,
    activist
Ken Campbell, writer, actor
George Carlin, comedian
Arthur C Clarke, writer
Beryl Cook, artist
Michael Crichton, writer
Mahmoud Darwish, poet
Bo Diddley, musician
Klaus Dinger, musician
Bobby Fischer, chess player
David Foster Wallace, writer
Dave Freeman, writer
*Grange Hill*, TV show
Gary Gygax, game designer
Jörg Haider, politician

Isaac Hayes, musician
Jesse Helms, politician
Charlton Heston, actor,
    activist
Edmund Hillary, mountaineer
Albert Hofmann, chemist
Pat Kavanagh, literary agent
Heath Ledger, actor
Humphrey Lyttelton,
    musician, broadcaster
Maharishi Mahesh Yogi, guru
Miriam Makeba, musician
Adrian Mitchell, poet
Paul Newman, actor
Bettie Page, model
Randy Pausch, writer,
    academic
Jacques Piccard, engineer,
    oceanographer
Harold Pinter, writer
Dorothy Podber,
    performance artist
Oliver Postgate, animator
Robert Rauschenberg, artist
Alain Robbe-Grillet, writer
Yves Saint Laurent, fashion
    designer
Roy Scheider, actor
Alexander Solzhenitsyn,
    writer, activist
Levi Stubbs, musician
Suharto, Indonesian ruler
Yma Sumac, musician

Jerry Wexler, record producer

Norman Whitfield, record producer

*The Wire*, TV show

## 2009

Henry Allingham, WWI veteran

Cory Aquino, politician

JG Ballard, writer

Augusto Boal, theatre director

Gordon Burn, writer

David Carradine, actor

Marilyn Chambers, actor

Walter Cronkite, journalist, broadcaster

Jonny Dollar, record producer

*ER*, TV show

Farrah Fawcett, actor

Marilyn French, writer

Clement Freud, journalist, broadcaster

Jade Goody, TV personality

Lux Interior, musician

Iz the Wiz, grafitti artist

Michael Jackson, musician

Jack Jones, union leader, activist

Ali Akbar Khan, musician

John Martyn, musician

Frank McCourt, writer

Patrick McGoohan, actor

John Mortimer, writer, barrister

Rajeev Motwani, computer scientist

Christopher Nolan, writer

Velupillai Prabhakaran, Tamil leader

Natasha Richardson, actor

Bobby Robson, football manager

The *Rocky Mountain News*

Setanta, sports broadcaster

Ron Silver, actor, activist

Neda Salehi Agha Soltan, student

Ivor Spencer, butler

Helen Suzman, politician

Ian Tomlinson, bystander

John Updike, writer

Steven Wells, journalist

# Thinking aloud

And finally, a few memorable quotes from the Noughties for your delight and delectation:

'There's no cave deep enough for America, or dark enough to hide.'
George W Bush

'Honestly, I think we should just trust our president in every decision that he makes, and we should just support that.'
Britney Spears

'I think that gay marriage is something that should be between a man and a woman.'
Arnold Schwarzenegger

'Voting Tory will cause your wife to have bigger breasts and increase your chances of owning a BMW M3.'
Boris Johnson

'I have benefited greatly from criticism, and at no time have I suffered a lack thereof.'
Donald Rumsfeld

'They think work is a four-letter word.'
Hillary Clinton

'Dumbledore is gay.'
JK Rowling

'In Iran, we don't have homosexuals.'
Mahmoud Ahmadinejad, President

'It is politically inconvenient to acknowledge what everyone knows; the Iraq War is largely about oil.'
Alan Greenspan

'Actresses have to be able to frown.'
Catherine Deneuve on Botox

'I'm such a Luddite. I can't even load a CD onto an iPod.'
Uma Thurman

'Some players have psychologists, some have sportologists. I smoke.'
Ángel Cabrera, golfer

'That wrinkly, white-haired guy used me in his campaign ad, which means I'm running for president. So thanks for the endorsement white-haired dude, and I want America to know I'm, like, totally ready to lead.'
Paris Hilton

'I want to see hedge-fund managers tipped into cage fights with naked gypsies.'
Matthew Parris, columnist for *The Times*

'The web is the most important book in the world.'
Jeff Bezos, founder of Amazon

'Whatever doesn't kill you simply makes you stranger.'
Heath Ledger as 'the Joker'

# Bibliography and further reading

Adams, Richard, *Watership Down* (London: Rex Collings, 1972)

Al Aswany, Alaa, *Chicago* (Translated by Farouk Abdel Wahab: London: Fourth Estate, 2007)

Ali, Rubina, *Slumgirl Dreaming* (London: Black Swan, 2009)

Amis, Martin, *The Second Plane: September 11, 2001–2007* (London: Jonathan Cape, 2008)

Anderson, Chris, *Free: The future of a radical price* (New York: Hyperion, 2009)

Anderson, Chris, *The Long Tail: Why the future of business is selling less of more* (New York: Hyperion, 2006)

Atwood, Margaret, *Payback: Debt and the shadow side of wealth* (Toronto: House of Anansi, 2008)

Atwood, Margaret, *The Year of the Flood* (London: Bloomsbury, 2009)

Backman, Michael, *Asian Eclipse: Exposing the dark side of business in Asia* (Singapore: John Wiley, 1999)

Baker, Stephen, *The Numerati* (New York: Houghton Mifflin, 2008)

Ballard, JG, *The Drowned World* (New York: Berkley, 1962)

Banks, Iain, *Dead Air* (London: Little, Brown: 2002)

Barber, Benjamin R, *Jihad vs McWorld: Terrorism's challenge to democracy* (New York: Ballantine, 1995)

Battelle, John, *The Search: How Google and its rivals rewrote the rules of business and transformed our culture* (New York: Portfolio, 2005)

Baudrillard, Jean, *The Intelligence of Evil or the Lucidity Pact* (Translated by Chris Turner: Oxford, UK: Berg, 2005)

Bayard, Pierre, *How To Talk About Books You Haven't Read* (Translated by Jeffrey Mehlman: New York: Bloomsbury, 2007)

Beigbeder, Frédéric, *Windows on the World: A novel* (Translated by Frank Wynne: London: Fourth Estate, 2004)

Borges, Jorge Luis, *Collected Fictions* (Translated by Andrew Hurley: New York: Viking, 1998)

Bova, Ben, *The Dueling Machine* (New York: Holt, Rinehart & Winston, 1969)

Boyle, David, *Authenticity: Brands, fakes, spin and the lust for real life* (London: Flamingo, 2003)

Brown, Dan, *The Da Vinci Code* (New York: Doubleday, 2003)

Bywater, Michael, *Lost Worlds: What have we lost & where did it go?* (London: Granta, 2004)

Carey, Peter, *Wrong About Japan* (London: Faber & Faber, 2005)

Carson, Rachel, *Silent Spring* (New York: Houghton Mifflin, 1962)

Chernow, Ron, *The Death of the Banker: The decline and fall of the great financial dynasties and the triumph of the small investor* (New York: Vintage, 1997)

Clake, Jacky (editor), *Britain in 2009* (Swindon, UK: ESRC, 2008)

Clark, Taylor, *Starbucked: A double tall tale of caffeine, commerce and culture* (New York: Little, Brown, 2007)

Cleave, Chris, *Incendiary* (London: Chatto & Windus, 2005)

Cooper, Lawrence, *The Cult of Celebrity: What our fascination with the stars reveals about us* (Boston: Skirt, 2009)

Coupland, Douglas, *JPod* (London: Bloomsbury, 2006)

Danziger, Pamela N, *Why People Buy Things They Don't Need: Understanding and predicting consumer behavior* (New York: Kaplan, 2004)

DeLillo, Don, *Falling Man: A novel* (New York: Scribner, 2007)

Dick, Philip K, *A Scanner Darkly* (New York: Doubleday, 1977)

Dixey, Anne, *United States of Hysteria: An Englishwoman's journey through the madness of America* (Wolvey, UK: Monday, 2008)

Donaton, Scott, *Madison & Vine: Why the entertainment and advertising industries must converge to survive* (New York: McGraw-Hill, 2004)

Eliot, TS, *The Complete Poems and Plays* (London: Faber & Faber, 1969)

Ellis, Bret Easton, *American Psycho* (New York: Vintage, 1991)

Faulks, Sebastian, *A Week in December* (London: Hutchinson, 2009)

Ferguson, Niall, *The Ascent of Money: A financial history of the world* (London: Allen Lane, 2008)

Fishburn, Dudley (editor), *The World in 2000* (London: Economist, 1999)

Foer, Jonathan Safran, *Extremely Loud and Incredibly Close: A novel* (Boston: Houghton Mifflin, 2005)

Footman, Tim, *Welcome to the Machine: OK Computer and the death of the classic album* (New Malden, UK: Chrome Dreams, 2007)

Franklin, Daniel (editor), *The World in 2009* (London: Economist, 2008)

Franzen, Jonathan, *The Corrections* (New York: Farrar, Straus & Giroux, 2001)

Frey, James, *A Million Little Pieces* (New York: Doubleday, 2003)

Friedman, Thomas, *Hot, Flat and Crowded: Why we need a green revolution – and how it can renew America* (New York: Farrar, Straus & Giroux, 2008)

Friedman, Thomas, *The Lexus and the Olive Tree: Understanding globalization* (New York: Farrar, Straus & Giroux, 1999)

Friedman, Thomas, *The World is Flat: A brief history of the twenty-first century* (New York: Farrar, Straus & Giroux, 2005)

Fukuyama, Francis, *The End of History and the Last Man* (New York: Free Press, 1992)

Galbraith, JK, *The Great Crash of 1929* (Boston: Houghton Mifflin, 1954)

Gibson, William, *Pattern Recognition* (New York: Putnam, 2003)

Gladwell, Malcolm, *Blink: The power of thinking without thinking* (New York: Little, Brown, 2005)

Gladwell, Malcolm, *The Tipping Point: How little things can make a big difference* (New York: Little Brown, 2000)

Gondry, Michel, *You'll Like This Film Because You're In It: The be kind rewind protocol* (New York: PictureBox, 2008)

Goody, Jade, *Jade: Fighting to the end* (London: John Blake, 2009)

Gray, John, *Al Qaeda and What it Means to be Modern* (London: Faber & Faber, 2003)

Hamid, Mohsin, *The Reluctant Fundamentalist* (London: Hamish Hamilton, 2007)

Hitori, Nakano, *Train Man: The story of the Train Man who fell in love with a girl, Hermes* (Translated by Bonnie Elliott: London: Robinson, 2006)

Holtzman, David H, *Privacy Lost: How technology is endangering your privacy* (Hoboken, NJ: Jossey-Bass, 2006)

Hornby, Nick, *High Fidelity: A novel* (London: Gollancz, 1995)

Hosseini, Khaled, *The Kite Runner* (London: Bloomsbury, 2003)

Houellebecq, Michel, *Platform* (Translated by Frank Wynne: London: Heinemann, 2002)

Ishikawa, Tetsuya, *How I Caused the Credit Crunch: An insider's story of the financial meltdown* (London: Icon, 2009)

Jacobs, AJ, *The Know-It-All: One man's humble quest to become the smartest person in the world* (New York: Simon & Schuster, 2004)

Jacobson, Sid and Ernie Colón, *The 9/11 Report: A graphic adaptation* (New York: Hill & Wang, 2006)

Jacques, Martin, *When China Rules the World: The rise of the middle kingdom and the end of the Western world* (London: Allen Lane, 2009)

James, Oliver, *Affluenza: How to be successful and stay sane* (London: Vermilion, 2007)

Johnson, Steven, *Everything Bad is Good for You: How popular culture is actually making us smarter* (New York: Riverhead, 2005)

Jones, Dylan, *iPod, Therefore I Am: A personal journey through music* (London: Weidenfeld & Nicolson, 2005)

Kalder, Daniel, *Lost Cosmonaut: Travels to the republics that tourism forgot* (London: Faber & Faber, 2006)

Kean, Thomas H and Lee H Hamilton, *The 9/11 Report: The National Commission on terrorist attacks upon the United States* (New York: St Martin's Press, 2004)

Keen, Andrew, *The Cult of the Amateur: How today's internet is killing our culture* (New York: Doubleday, 2007)

Kinsella, Sophie, *The Secret Dreamworld of a Shopaholic* (London: Black Swan, 2000)

Klein, Naomi, *No Logo: Taking aim at the brand bullies* (Toronto: Knopf, 2000)

Klein, Naomi, *The Shock Doctrine: The rise of disaster capitalism* (Toronto: Knopf, 2007)

Krugman, Paul, *The Return of Depression Economics and the Crisis of 2008* (New York: WW Norton, 2008)

Lacy, Sarah, *The Stories of Facebook, YouTube & MySpace: The people, the hype and the deals behind the giants of Web 2.0* (London: Crimson, 2008)

Lasn, Kalle, *Culture Jam: How to reverse America's suicidal consumer binge – and why we must* (New York: Quill, 2000)

Lawson, Neal, *All Consuming: How shopping got us into this mess and how we can find our way out* (London: Penguin, 2009)

Leonard, Mark, *What Does China Think?* (London: Fourth Estate, 2008)

Levitt, Steven D and Stephen J Dubner, *Freakonomics: A rogue economist explores the hidden side of everything* (New York: William Morrow, 2005)

Lindstrom, Martin, *Buyology: How everything we believe about why we buy is wrong* (London: Random House, 2008)

Lloyd, John and John Mitchinson, *The Book of General Ignorance* (London: Faber & Faber, 2006)

Lomborg, Bjørn, *Cool It: The skeptical environmentalist's guide to global warming* (New York: Knopf, 2007)

Lynas, Mark, *Six Degrees: Our future on a hotter planet* (London: Fourth Estate, 2007)

MacKay, David, *Sustainable Energy: Without the hot air* (Cambridge, UK: UIT, 2008)

Mahbubani, Kishore, *The New Asian Hemisphere: The irresistible shift of global power to the East* (New York: Public Affairs, 2008)

McCarthy, Cormac, *The Road* (Toronto: Knopf, 2006)

McCreary, Sunny, *My Godawful Life: Abandoned. Betrayed. Stuck to the window* (London: Boxtree, 2008)

McEwan, Ian, *Saturday* (London: Jonathan Cape, 2005)

Meyer, Stephenie, *Twilight* (New York: Little, Brown, 2005)

Micklethwait, John and Adrian Wooldridge, *The Right Nation: Conservative power in America* (New York: Penguin, 2004)

Monbiot, George, *Heat: How to stop the planet burning* (London: Allen Lane, 2006)

Moore, Michael, *Stupid White Men...and Other Sorry Excuses for the State of the Nation* (Revised edition. London: Penguin, 2002)

Morley, Paul, *Words and Music: A history of pop in the shape of a city* (London: Bloomsbury, 2003)

Nicholls, David, *Starter for Ten* (London: Flame, 2003)

Obama, Barack, *The Audacity of Hope: Thoughts on reclaiming the American Dream* (New York: Crown, 2006)

O'Hara, Kieron and Nigel Shadbolt, *The Spy in the Coffee Machine: The end of privacy as we know it* (Oxford, UK: One World, 2008)

O'Neill, Joseph, *Netherland* (London: Fourth Estate, 2008)

Orwell, George, *Nineteen Eighty-Four* (London: Secker & Warburg, 1949)

Pelevin, Victor, *The Helmet of Horror: The myth of Theseus and the minotaur* (Translated by Andrew Bromfield: New York: Canongate, 2006)

Petit, Philippe, *To Reach the Clouds: My high wire walk between the twin towers* (New York: North Point Press, 2002)

Phillips, Melanie, *Londonistan* (London: Gibson Square, 2006)

Plato, *The Symposium* (Translated by Christopher Gill: London: Penguin, 2003)

Poole, Steven, *Unspeak™: The language of everyday deception* (London: Little, Brown, 2006)

Pyke, Magnus, *Our Future: Dr Magnus Pyke predicts* (Feltham, UK: Hamlyn, 1980)

Quinn, Bill, *How Wal-Mart is Destroying America (and the world) and What You Can Do About it* (Berkeley, CA: Ten Speed Press, 2000)

Rivoli, Pietra, *The Travels of a T-Shirt in the Global Economy: An economist examines the markets, power and politics of world trade* (Revised edition. Hoboken, NJ: John Wiley, 2009)

Robb, John, *The Nineties: What the f**k was that all about?* (London: Ebury, 1999)

Rowling, JK, *Harry Potter and the Deathly Hallows* (London: Bloomsbury, 2007)

Ruiz Zafón, Carlos, *The Shadow of the Wind* (Translated by Lucia Graves: New York: Penguin, 2004)

Rushdie, Salman, *The Satanic Verses* (London: Viking, 1988)

Sachs, Jeffrey, *The End of Poverty: Economic possibilities for our time* (New York: Penguin, 2005)

Sardar, Ziauddin and Merryl Wyn Davies, *Why Do People Hate America?* (Cambridge, UK: Icon, 2002)

Schumacher, EF, *Small is Beautiful: Economics as if people mattered* (New York: Harper & Row, 1973)

Simms, Andrew and Petra Kjell and Ruth Potts, *Clone Town Britain: The survey results on the bland state of the nation* (London: New Economics Foundation, 2005)

Simms, Andrew, *Tescopoly: How one shop came out on top and why it matters* (London: Constable, 2007)

Sinclair, Iain, *Sorry Meniscus: Excursions to the Millennium Dome* (London: Profile, 1999)

Sterling, Bruce, *Tomorrow Now: Envisioning the next 50 years* (New York: Random House, 2002)

Stross, Randall, *Planet Google: One company's audacious plan to organize everything we know* (New York: Free Press, 2008)

Swarup, Vikas, *Q & A: A novel* (New York: Scribner, 2005)

Toledo, Camille de, *Coming of Age at the End of History* (Translated by Blake Ferris: New York: Soft Skull Press, 2008)

Tolkien, JRR, *The Lord of the Rings* (Originally published as three books in 1954–1955 by Allen & Unwin, London. Republished London: HarperCollins, 1995)

Truss, Lynne, *Eats Shoots & Leaves: The zero tolerance approach to punctuation* (London: Profile, 2003)

Updike, John, *Terrorist: A novel* (New York: Knopf, 2006)

Wheen, Francis, *How Mumbo-Jumbo Conquered the World: A short history of modern delusions* (London: Harper Perennial, 2004)

Winchester, Simon, *The Meaning of Everything: The story of the Oxford English Dictionary* (Oxford, UK: OUP, 2003)

Wolfe, Tom, *The Bonfire of the Vanities* (New York: Bantam, 1987)

Wright, Evan, *Generation Kill: Devil dogs, Iceman, Captain America and the new face of American war* (New York: Putnam, 2004)

Zakaria, Fareed, *The Post-American World* (New York: WW Norton, 2008)

Zamyatin, Yevgeny, *We* (Originally written in 1921. Translated by Clarence Brown: New York: Penguin, 1993)

# Notes

1. Ferdinand Mount, 'The doctrine of unripe time', the *London Review of Books*, November 16, 2006. See also Dominic Sandbrook, 'Why we love history in 10-year chapters', the *Observer*, April 19, 2009.
2. As outlined by the philosopher and political economist Francis Fukuyama in *The End of History and the Last Man* (New York: Free Press, 1992). Fukuyama's contention was that, with the fall of communism, liberal democracy would become the *de facto* mode of governance across the world. As the author later graciously acknowledged, he hadn't properly taken into account the power of political Islamism; as another renowned commentator might have put it, 'D'oh!'
3. Stephen Moss, 'The history makers', the *Guardian*, May 26, 2009.
4. The 1980s equivalent is that shot of a 'yuppie' (young upwardly-mobile professional) juggling his Filofax in an infuriating manner.
5. Michael Bywater, *Lost Worlds: What have we lost & where did it go?* (London: Granta, 2004) p.164.
6. 'The Book of Revelation', Chapter 20, verse 3.
7. Christopher Farrell, 'Why the burst internet bubble didn't break the economy', *BusinessWeek*, July 21, 2000.
8. Stephen Bayley, 'A decade on...the Dome finally works', the *Observer*, June 24, 2007. The Dome was eventually reopened as the O2 Arena, a hugely successful venue for concerts and other events.
9. Beyond the English-speaking world, political life was rather more exciting in the 1990s. Italy got its first brief taste of Silvio Berlusconi (who was prime minister in the middle of the decade), while the erratic behaviour of Russia's President Boris Yeltsin at least drew attention away from that country's loss of power and prestige following the dismantling of the Soviet Union.

10. Frédéric Beigbeder, *Windows on the World: A novel* (Translated by Frank Wynne: London: Fourth Estate, 2004) p.63.

11. Thomas H Kean and Lee H Hamilton, *The 9/11 Report: The National Commission on terrorist attacks upon the United States* (New York: St Martin's Press, 2004) p.LXXXI.

12. On a personal note, I was at an exhibition of architectural models at the British Museum in London on September 11. By chance, I was standing in front of a model of the World Trade Center when I took a call informing me of the news.

13. See also Ziauddin Sardar and Merryl Wyn Davies, *Why Do People Hate America?* (Cambridge, UK: Icon, 2002) p.5.

14. Captain America was originally conceived (pre-Marvel) as a hero battling against another threat to American liberty, the Nazis.

15. Duncan Campbell, '"Dixie sluts" fight on with naked defiance', the *Guardian*, April 25, 2003.

16. In 1966, the Beatle gave an interview to a London newspaper in which he declared that his band was 'more popular than Jesus'. When his remarks were reprinted in a US magazine it led to protests, boycotts, death threats and the public burning of Beatles records and memorabilia. Only a public apology defused the situation.

17. Mark Binelli, 'A man for our time', *Rolling Stone*, August 10, 2006.

18. Rebecca Allison, '9/11 wicked but a work of art, says Damien Hirst', the *Guardian*, September 11, 2002.

19. Michael Moore, *Stupid White Men…and Other Sorry Excuses for the State of the Nation* (Revised edition. London: Penguin, 2002) p.xii.

20. Frédéric Beigbeder, *Windows on the World: A novel* (Translated by Frank Wynne: London: Fourth Estate, 2004) p.60.

21. King Kong had fought with the biplanes on top of the Empire State Building in the legendary 1933 movie; the World Trade Center was the setting for the dismal 1976 remake.

22. Iain Banks, *Dead Air* (London: Little, Brown, 2002) p.24.

23. 'Windows on the world', *The Economist*, May 19, 2005.

24. Ed Pilkington and Andrew Clark, 'Manhattan plane crash reawakens spectre of 9/11', the *Guardian*, October 12, 2006.

25. 'Attacks draw mixed response in Mideast', cnn.com, September 12, 2001.

26. See George W Bush's 2002 'State of the Union' address.

27. Martin Amis, *The Second Plane: September 11, 2001–2007* (London: Jonathan Cape, 2008) p.139.

28. As US Defense Secretary Donald Rumsfeld helpfully explained in a June 6, 2002 press conference at NATO headquarters in Brussels; 'There's another way to phrase that and that is that the absence of evidence is not the evidence of absence. It is basically saying the same thing in a different way. Simply because you do not have evidence that something exists does not mean that you have evidence that it doesn't exist.'

29. Laura Miller, 'The salon interview: Ian McEwan', salon.com, April 9, 2005.

30. This is the incident that brought to prominence the baggage handler John Smeaton, who subdued one of the terrorists. His subsequent comment, 'This is Glasgow. We'll just set aboot ye!', was enough to make him a media celebrity for a brief while.

31. Giuliani tried to parlay his success and popularity into a bid for the Republican presidential nomination in 2008; it turned out to be one of the dampest political squibs of the decade.

32. Department of Defense news briefing, October 7, 2002.

33. 'Guantánamo commander says three detainees hang themselves with makeshift nooses', *USA Today*, June 11, 2006.

34. Of the developed regions, Australia is set to be particularly badly hit by climate change. In December 2008, it was announced that the country's driest state, South Australia (the state capital of which is Adelaide), had been forced to purchase water for the first time to ensure adequate supplies after a five-year drought. Karlene Maywald, the state's Minister for Water Security, remarked; 'We're just being prudent, getting into the market and buying it [water] to make sure we've got it.'

35. Randeep Ramesh, 'India won't accept emissions limits, says climate envoy', the *Guardian*, December 8, 2008.

36. This backdoor lobbying is described in Steven Poole's *Unspeak™: The language of everyday deception* (London: Little, Brown, 2006) pp.42–49.
37. Leo Hickman, 'Are rock tours bad for the environment?', the *Guardian*, October 18, 2006.
38. In his article 'Civilization ends with a shutdown of human concern' (the *Guardian*, October 30, 2007), environmental campaigner George Monbiot described it as 'the most important environmental book ever written'.
39. 'The planet is now so vandalized that only total energy renewal can save us', the *Guardian*, November 25, 2008.
40. Duncan Clark, 'Maldives first to go carbon-neutral', the *Observer*, March 15, 2009.
41. From his speech delivered at the annual 'TED' conference in Monterey, California, 2007.
42. See Chapter 7. Also Pamela N Danziger's *Why People Buy Things They Don't Need: Understanding and predicting consumer behavior* (New York: Kaplan, 2004) p.2, in which she describes concern about the social and environmental impact of excessive consumption as 'strangely un-American'.
43. Scott Donaton, *Madison & Vine: Why the entertainment and advertising industries must converge to survive* (New York: McGraw-Hill, 2004) pp.49–60.
44. Ben Goldacre, 'Quacks, hacks and pressing problems with press releases', the *Guardian*, May 30, 2009.
45. Although some (for example, *Blender*) later reappeared online.
46. Vampires were big in the Noughties, especially with teenage girls. Stephenie Meyer's *Twilight* series of novels (first published in 2005), and the inevitable movie adaptation, picked up where Buffy left off. The British comedy horror *Lesbian Vampire Killers* (2009) was rather less successful.
47. In August/September 2006, the counter-culture artist Banksy replaced up to 500 copies of Paris Hilton's debut CD, *Paris*, in 48

different UK record stores with his own cover art and remixes by Danger Mouse. Music tracks were given titles such as 'Why Am I Famous?', 'What Have I Done?' and 'What Am I For?' Several copies of the CD were purchased by the public before stores were able to remove them, some going on to be sold for as much as £750 through online auction sites such as eBay.

48. Racially-insensitive indiscretions were a very Noughties phenomenon; see also Michael 'Kramer' Richards, Mel Gibson, Prince Harry *et al.*

49. The British journalist John Diamond had also discussed the progress of his cancer in public, via his weekend column in *The Times* newspaper and on television. But this was in the 1990s, before blogging and social networking added a whole new dimension to the word 'public'.

50. Nick Cullen, 'Sir Michael Parkinson: "Jade Goody was a wretched role model"', *The Times*, April 7, 2009.

51. Michael Bywater, *Lost Worlds: What have we lost & where did it go?* (London: Granta, 2004) p.13.

52. Judith Woods, 'Avatars and Second Life adultery: A tale of online cheating and real-world heartbreak', the *Daily Telegraph*, November 14, 2008.

53. David Boyle, *Authenticity: Brands, fakes, spin and the lust for real life* (London: Flamingo, 2003) p.155.

54. Although the first recorded use of 'Google' as a verb was by the company's co-founder, Larry Page, back on July 8, 1998 (when he wrote on a mailing list 'Have fun and keep Googling!'), Google consistently discouraged use of the word in this way. In October 2006, the company issued a plea to members of the public; 'You should please only use "Google" when you're actually referring to Google Inc and our services.'

55. Initially hailed as an audacious move by business analysts, by June 2009 (with both its popularity and advertising revenue plummeting) MySpace had announced redundancies as part of an efficiency drive.

56. See also Chris Anderson's book *Free: The future of a radical price* (New York: Hyperion, 2009).

57. Again, something prefigured by cinema. It could be argued that Gaspar Noé's film *Irréversible* (2002), which begins with the aftermath of a revenge attack, then works back scene by scene to unpick the outrage that provoked it, is an early example of blog chronology in another medium.

58. Sarah Lacy, *The Stories of Facebook, YouTube & MySpace: The people, the hype and the deals behind the giants of Web 2.0* (London: Crimson, 2008) p.110.

59. Brad Stone and Noam Cohen, 'Social networks spread defiance online', the *New York Times*, June 15, 2009.

60. Paul Boutin, 'Twitter, Flickr, Facebook make blogs look so 2004', *Wired*, November 2008.

61. Andrew Keen, *The Cult of the Amateur: How today's internet is killing our culture* (New York: Doubleday, 2007) p.37.

62. Nicholas Carr, 'Is Google making us stupid?', the *Atlantic*, July/ August 2008.

63. Siobhain Butterworth, 'Open door', the *Guardian*, May 4, 2009.

64. See Chapter 8; also Dylan Jones, *iPod, Therefore I Am: A personal journey through music* (London: Weidenfeld & Nicholson, 2005) and Tim Footman, *Welcome to the Machine: OK Computer and the death of the classic album* (New Malden, UK: Chrome Dreams, 2007) pp.246–263.

65. The internet in China is highly policed and regulated by what is known as 'the Great Firewall of China'. The firewall blocks particular IP addresses, domain names and key words, for example Falun Gong, an illegal spiritual group. In June 2009, the 20th anniversary of the Tiananmen Square massacre, access to Twitter, Hotmail and other sites was temporarily suspended.

66. Thomas H Kean and Lee H Hamilton, *The 9/11 Report: The National Commission on terrorist attacks upon the United States* (New York: St Martin's Press, 2004) p.538.

67. Kathryn Flett, 'The un-Cheryl of the world', the *Observer*, May 3, 2009.

68. More properly, the 'USA PATRIOT Act' (an unwieldy acronym for Uniting and Strengthening America by Providing Appropriate Tools Required to Intercept and Obstruct Terrorism).

69. Polly Toynbee, 'Surveillance: Social benefit or genuine menace?' Edited by Jacky Clake, *Britain in 2009* (Swindon, UK: ESRC, 2008) p.48.

70. In October 2008, London's Westminster City Council announced that the artwork 'One Nation Under CCTV' by counter-culturalist Banksy would be painted over as it was graffiti. Stating that it would remove any graffiti (regardless of the reputation of its creator), the work was duly obliterated in April 2009.

71. This was brought home to Google in 2005 (a few months after Google Maps was released) when Elinor Mills, a reporter for CNET News, revealed a number of personal details about Google CEO Eric Schmidt; details she had picked up from the eponymous search engine.

72. Ben Evans, 'GOP [Grand Old Party] drops efforts to rename Democrats "socialist"', Associated Press, May 20, 2009.

73. In the mid-Noughties, 'the hoodie' became a conflation of the banal and the demonic – at once a nondescript garment and the stereotypical wearer of one, an anti-social, knife-carrying yob. The suggestion by the British Conservative leader David Cameron that we should be more understanding of hoodies (2006) attracted much derision, but signalled a more inclusive aspect to 21st-century Toryism.

74. In fact, drivers throughout the decade were forced to consider such apparent contradictions. In Europe, some local authorities introduced congestion charges to discourage private cars from city centres. At the same time, others experimented with the removal of speed limits and traffic lights to encourage the free movement of vehicles. In July 2009, the English town of Swindon scrapped its permanent speed cameras.

75. Bruce Sterling, *Tomorrow Now: Envisioning the next 50 years* (New York: Random House, 2002) p.175.

76. The social networking site Facebook faced a storm of protest in 2009 when it seemingly changed its terms of service to retain perpetual rights over users' photographs, wall posts, comments and other data. Promoted as a way of ensuring that users could access this material even if its originators had deleted their account, users took the move as a huge blow to their privacy rights.

77. 'A nation challenged: Excerpts from the President's remarks on the War on Terrorism', the *New York Times*, October 12, 2001.

78. Taylor Clark, *Starbucked: A double tall tale of caffeine, commerce and culture* (New York: Little, Brown, 2007) p.259.

79. In 2005, Exeter, an ancient cathedral city in south-west England, had the unwelcome distinction of having its high street named the most homogeneous in Britain by the New Economics Foundation (in its *Clone Town Britain* survey), boasting only one independent retailer, a tobacconist. Meanwhile, just 20 miles down the road, the pretty market town of Totnes became the first in the UK to issue its own currency – the 'Totnes pound' – to support its diverse local economy.

80. Andrew Simms, *Tescopoly: How one shop came out on top and why it matters* (London: Constable, 2007) p.169.

81. Ben Summerskill, 'Shopping can make you depressed', the *Observer*, May 6, 2001.

82. Clark, p.266.

83. Michael Bywater, *Lost Worlds: What have we lost & where did it go?* (London: Granta, 2004) p.38.

84. Andrew J Bacevich, 'He told us to go shopping. Now the bill is due', the *Washington Post*, October 5, 2008.

85. In May 2009 (following a successful release in Canada), *RiP: A remix manifesto*, a feature-length documentary about copyright and music in an online world, opened in New York. Siding with those who borrow freely from existing art to make their own, its

director (Brett Gaylor) made the entire film available to watch online *gratis*. The main focus of the film is the mash-up artist Girl Talk; a particular highlight being the scene where Marybeth Peters, the US Registrar of Copyrights, is visibly impressed by footage of Girl Talk's cut and paste studio techniques, but then still asserts; 'You can't argue your creativity when it's based on other people's stuff.'

86. In April 2009, four members of Pirate Bay were handed down prison terms and fines by the Swedish courts. In a blog post message on its website, Pirate Bay called the verdict 'a little speedbump' on the information superhighway and appealed the sentence.

87. Launched one month after 9/11, the iPod is a good measure of the extent to which technological developments divide history into discrete segments, 9/11 being 'BiP' (Before iPod). Nobody who died in the Twin Towers would ever know the thrill of the scroll wheel; none would join the club signified by those little white headphones.

88. This exposure was interrupted in Britain for a while. In March 2009, YouTube started blocking certain music videos on its UK site after failing to reach a new licensing agreement with the Performing Rights Society.

89. Peter Shapiro, 'Criminal elements', *The Wire*, April 2002.

90. Eric Steuer, 'The infinite album', *Wired*, September 2006.

91. Andrew Collins, 'Wan love', *The Word,* October 2006.

92. *Paul Morley's Guide to Musical Genres*, BBC Radio 2, June 3, 2008. In the same programme, English alternative rock musician Billy Bragg described emo as 'soft-focus goth' and Stuart Braithwaite of post-rockers Mogwai called it 'American radio rock with sideways haircuts'. Cruel, but Morley's accusation of meaningless is probably closer to the truth. Incidentally, none of the bands that spoke to Morley would admit to being emo.

93. Dylan Jones, *iPod, Therefore I Am: A personal journey through music* (London: Weidenfeld & Nicolson, 2005) p.61.

94. This phrase achieved popularity in English through its use in the film *Slumdog Millionaire*.

95. The term was coined (as *'le tiers monde'*) in 1952 by a French demographer, Alfred Sauvy. 'Developing world' is now the preferred expression.

96. Josef Joffe, 'The new new world', the *New York Times*, May 11, 2008. See also Fareed Zakaria, *The Post-American World* (New York: WW Norton, 2008).

97. 'With friends like these. . .', the *Washington Post*, April 18, 2006.

98. *Slumdog Millionaire* was actually a British production, albeit one set and shot entirely in India. The film's success (it won the 2008 Oscar for Best Picture) provoked accusations of cultural insensitivity and exploitation, as its young stars were plucked from the Mumbai slums and exposed to the glitz of Hollywood. Questions were raised about the extent to which these youngsters should share in the financial success of the film; a microcosm of the possibilities and perils of a globalized cultural economy. In 2009, Rubina Ali, who played the young Latika, published her autobiography. She was nine years old.

99. Pietra Rivoli, *The Travels of a T-Shirt in the Global Economy: An economist examines the markets, power and politics of world trade* (Revised edition. Hoboken, NJ: John Wiley, 2009) pp.227–238.

100. Frédéric Beigbeder, *Windows on the World: A novel* (Translated by Frank Wynne: London: Fourth Estate, 2004) p.222.

101. A neologism from the 1930s that found a new lease of life in 2008. See also Ron Chernow, *The Death of the Banker: The decline and fall of the great financial dynasties and the triumph of the small investor* (New York: Vintage, 1997).

102. Britain's deregulatory 'Big Bang' of 1986 prompted an explosion in financial services. In 2007, a staggering £2.15 trillion of capital flowed into the UK, some £295 billion more than the US.

103. John Lanchester, 'It's finished', the *London Review of Books*, May 28, 2009.

104. Not that Stewart seemed to have had much influence on the underlying culture. When I went to the *Daily Show* website to watch the video of his confrontation with Cramer, there was a banner advertising an online MBA course. Money, it seemed, still talked.
105. 'A nation at war; Rumsfeld's words on Iraq: "There is untidiness"', the *New York Times*, April 12, 2003.
106. Rachel Cooke, 'Making great drama out of a credit crisis', the *Observer*, May 10, 2009.
107. From Tom Wolfe's 1987 novel *The Bonfire of the Vanities*, the term referring to the book's bond salesman anti-hero Sherman McCoy.
108. TS Eliot, *The Complete Poems and Plays* (London: Faber & Faber, 1969). Burnt Norton is the name of a manor house in Gloucestershire that Eliot visited in 1934.
109. Some readers might also remember Dr Pyke from his cameo performance on Thomas Dolby's 1982 hit single 'She Blinded Me with Science'.
110. For more 'futures that never were', check out the website www.paleofuture.com.
111. Jorge Luis Borges, *Collected Fictions* (Translated by Andrew Hurley: New York: Viking, 1998), p.325.
112. Guilty.
113. Back to what I was saying about the fractured canon. If I had made references to Plato's *Symposium* and the Tower of Babel 100 years ago, I could have been pretty certain that the majority of readers would have understood them. Now I could be pretty certain that, if you didn't immediately understand them, you soon would, having looked them up on Google.
114. Ken Hollings, 'Dawn of the replicants', *The Wire*, September 2000. The Italian creators of 'Luther Blissett' appropriated his name from a British footballer who played briefly (and without much success) for AC Milan in the 1980s.
115. Jim Crace, 'A new kind of ghost writer', the *Guardian*, October 28, 2006.